Frank Scurry

NEW TESTAMENT GUIDES

General .

A.T. Linc

JOHN

**Please Return To
Frank P. Scurry**

JOHN

Barnabas Lindars, SSF

jsot press

Published by JSOT Press
JSOT Press is an imprint of
Sheffield Academic Press Ltd
343 Fulwood Road
Sheffield S10 3BP
England

Typeset by
Sheffield Academic Press
and
Printed on acid-free paper in Great Britain
by The Cromwell Press
Melksham, Wiltshire

British Library Cataloguing in Publication Data

Lindars, Barnabas
    John
    1. Bible. N.T. John
    I. Title   II. Series
    226.5

    ISSN 0959-9401
    ISBN 1-85075-255-9

CONTENTS

Commentaries on John

Commentaries on the Gospel of John are legion. The reader is advised to buy one good commentary, and to work through the Gospel with it systematically. The following short selection gives commentaries which either do not require knowledge of Greek on the part of the reader or can be used without difficulty by those who have no knowledge of Greek:

G. R. Beasley-Murray, Word Biblical Commentary, Waco: Word, 1987. The most recent large commentary.
R. E. Brown, The Anchor Commentary, 2 vols., Garden City: Doubleday, 1966-70. One of the best commentaries currently available.
B. Lindars, New Century Bible, London: Oliphants, 1972. Widely used in colleges and schools, and accessible to non-specialist readers.
J. Marsh, Pelican Gospel Commentaries, Harmondsworth: Penguin, 1968. Straightforward, but lacking in detail.
J. N. Sanders and B. A. Mastin, Black's New Testament Commentaries, London: A. & C. Black, 1968. An exposition in running commentary.
R. Schnackenburg, Herders Theological Commentary on the New Testament, 3 vols., London: Burns & Oates, 1968, 1980, 1982. Long, but very highly recommended for balanced discussion of major issues.

The following require knowledge of Greek:

C. K. Barrett, London: SPCK, [2]1978. Very good on text and language.
J. H. Bernard, The International Critical Commentary, 2 vols., Edinburgh: T. & T. Clark, 1928. Old, but still useful.

R. Bultmann, Oxford: Blackwell, 1971. A highly individual interpretation, which has had profound influence on modern study of John.

Other commentaries which are notable for the authors' interpretation of the Fourth Gospel are:

E. Haenchen, Hermeneia, 2. vols., Philadelphia: Fortress, 1984. A commentary along similar lines to that of Bultmann.
E. C. Hoskyns and F. N. Davey, London: Faber & Faber, [2]1947. Strong grasp of theological issues.
B. F. Westcott, London: Murray, [2]1881 (on English text); 2 vols., 1908 (on Greek text). A classic, both conservative and imaginative.

1

ORIENTATION

A Gospel of Surprises

IF THE GOSPEL OF JOHN had been the only account we possessed of the life of Jesus, we might still be fascinated and intrigued by it, and we might even wonder whether it could possibly be true. But the problems which it presents would not be so complex and difficult as they become when it is read as the last of four Gospels, all purporting to describe the same thing. To read John straight after the others cannot fail to reveal vast differences. John starts with a philosophical statement (1.1-18), which has no counterpart in the Synoptic Gospels. Then comes the witness of John the Baptist (1.19-34). This may suggest a move into familiar territory, in spite of the very different presentation from the Synoptic parallels. But this hope is quickly shattered by the call of the first disciples (1.35-51), which has virtually nothing in common with the Synoptic accounts (e.g. Mark 1.16-20; Luke 5.1-11), and indeed seems irreconcilable with them. This problem of the relation to the Synoptic Gospels continues through to the end.

At the same time a reading of John shows also differences of style. After the first two chapters, and the surprise caused by discovering the Cleansing of the Temple (2.13-22) before the ministry of Jesus has even begun, instead of near the end, the narrative ceases to be episodic and gives way to long discourses and debates of Jesus in Jerusalem, which are completely different from the Synoptic Gospels. The difference extends beyond the literary form to the effect which is produced. Here Jesus emerges as a remote personality, almost wholly taken up with the subject of his personal authority in relation to God. The story of Jesus has been shifted onto a different plane with a new centre of interest.

Though John's picture of Jesus has important points of contact with the earlier tradition, there is a very pronounced change of emphasis. Jesus' awareness of an intimate relation with God, whom he addresses as 'Father' (e.g. Matt. 11.25-27), becomes in John an insistent theme. Jesus constantly calls himself 'the Son' in a way that implies christological significance, equivalent to the less frequent designations 'Son of God' and 'Son of man'. There is a similar change in the claim of Jesus that he has been 'sent' by God. In the Synoptic Gospels the idea refers to Jesus' prophetic vocation (e.g. Matt. 10.40), like the prophets of old or John the Baptist, who was also 'sent' according to John 1.6. But the idea is applied to Jesus in John in a more fundamental sense. John gives a distinct impression that Jesus is a heavenly emissary from God, who has been sent down to earth and then returns after his work on earth is done (cf. John 17.1-5). As Wayne Meeks has pointed out in a celebrated article, this raises not only the problem of the pre-existence of Jesus, but also the question whether John is indebted to a myth of a descending and ascending heavenly emissary, and if so where it comes from. Evidently John's understanding of the person and work of Jesus differs from the Synoptic tradition.

This different understanding in its turn raises further problems, which can be grouped under the headings of history, reception and influence.

History in John

It is already clear that there is a disconcerting lack of agreement between John and the Synoptics on matters of history. Further examples can easily be found. Many attempts have been made to harmonise these discrepancies. It has even been suggested that Jesus did his dramatic action of cleansing the temple twice over. Such a suggestion is surely a counsel of despair.

This is only one level of the historical problem. A deeper question is posed by the presentation of Jesus himself. The

Gospel of John has played an immensely important part in the formulation of Christian doctrine, because of the statements which Jesus makes about himself, suggesting that he is the Son of God in a unique sense. From such statements Christian tradition has asserted that Jesus is the incarnate Son of God, both human and divine. We may well ask how far this represents what the evangelist intended to convey? The question warns us to be on our guard against presupposing too easily that the christological statements in John mean exactly the same as the later definitions.

But behind that there is the more disturbing question whether Jesus actually said the things that are attributed to him in the Fourth Gospel. Has the later construction of Christian doctrine been built on claims attributed to Jesus which he never made at all, and might well have repudiated if he had known about them? It is this kind of question which makes the problem of the historical value of the Gospel so acute.

Questions of this kind are not merely historical questions. They raise the whole problem of hermeneutics, that is, the proper way to understand the Fourth Gospel and its meaning for today. If Jesus in the Fourth Gospel poses the question of his identity to his opponents, it is inevitable that the Gospel puts the same question to the readers, and still does so today.

Reception

Most scholars agree that chapter 21 is an appendix to the Gospel. The original ending came at 20.30-31, in which the readers are addressed directly, and the purpose of the Gospel, to enable faith in Jesus as Christ and Son of God, is expressly stated. So the evangelist has an audience in mind for whom this unique account of Jesus may be expected to be meaningful. One reason, then, for the differences from the Synoptics is likely to be the special character of the people for whom it was written.

Consequently these differences can be used to determine the nature of the expected readership. At the very least, the Prologue suggests that the readers include people who would wish to relate the Gospel's claims concerning Jesus to a philosophical account of the nature of God and cosmology. This could imply a Greek or Gnostic readership. But it will also turn out that the disputes of Jesus in Jerusalem, which form the bulk of chapters 3–12, are concerned with issues between Christians and Jews opposed to them at the time when relations between church and synagogue had reached breaking-point. This suggests that the readers are actually involved in such disputes.

Considerations of this kind have led to various proposals concerning the identity of the readership. The important point is that the Gospel has been written in such a way as to speak to their condition. It is thus possible to identify broadly various groups to whom this might apply, such as Jewish-Christians, Gentile Christians, Jews in Palestine or the Diaspora, proto-Gnostics and pagan Greeks. They are people, each with their own traditions and ideology, with whom it may be supposed that John has 'relations' (to use a happily neutral word suggested by Beasley-Murray).

Influences

The idea that the evangelist writes for some or all of these groups presupposes that John is familiar with their religious concepts and knows how to make the gospel message meaningful to their situation. Some scholars would go further and try to prove that John was actually indebted to the ideology of such a group. This was the assumption of the History-of-Religions school, and is especially associated with the interpretation of Rudolf Bultmann. It is the kind of suggestion that can be very upsetting to modern readers, who feel that their confidence in the Fourth Gospel as a genuinely Christian book and an authentic record of Jesus is being undermined. It is thus all the more important to make a determined effort to discover the truth about John by careful and objective study, and to be ready to approach all these questions with an open mind.

Many Dimensions

The Gospel of John is deceptively simple in style and vocabulary. But it also has a mysterious quality, suggesting hidden depths. The reader is alerted at the outset that the story of Jesus is the crucial manifestation of a cosmic struggle between light and darkness (1.5). Thus the story operates at two levels, and the facts which are described also have symbolic meaning in relation to the theology of John. The historic circumstances of Jesus in his time are the stage on which the ultimate cosmic drama is played out. Jesus' victory (16.33) is not just a personal triumph, but the act in which the light finally overcomes the darkness and God's plan of salvation for all humanity is achieved.

At the same time there is another dimension. Though the readers are rarely addressed directly (but cf. 20.31), the Gospel challenges them to a decision all the way through. The Fourth Gospel is not episodic, like the Synoptics, but carefully planned with a series of set pieces, each leading up to a dramatic climax. The presentation is controlled by the skillful use of dialogue, or dramatic monologue, to engage the readers on the side of Jesus and to confront them personally with the decision which is set before Jesus' audience in the play. John's writing has perennial power, and challenges the modern reader still.

False Expectations

These preliminary considerations have given some idea of the scope of study of John. But a word of warning is desirable about the danger of approaching John with false expectations. In the first place, the multi-dimensional character of the Gospel obviously precludes the idea that it is a straight historical record of what actually happened and what Jesus actually said in his ministry. It is a mistake to suppose that there was any direct reporting of Jesus in his earthly life. The Synoptic Gospels are based on a variety of traditions, some oral and some written, which embodied the memories of people who knew Jesus, and evolved over a long period. Similarly John is dependent on the work of predecessors, and it should not be assumed that the underlying materials were substantially different from those used by the Synoptic writers.

It may be urged that this judgment does not allow for the claim within the Gospel itself that it was written by an eye-witness, described as 'the disciple whom Jesus loved' (21.20, 24). More will have to be said about this later. For the moment it must simply be asserted that, even if some element of eye-witness testimony has been incorporated in the Gospel, it does not have the status of a contemporary report of what was seen or heard. In so far as personal memories were available, they were memories of events long since past, which had inevitably been affected to some extent by later reflection in the light of the rise of Christianity. Moreover the evangelist used them creatively to produce a multi-dimensional and highly dramatic presentation of the tradition, in which all were adapted for the aim in view.

This also means that the hope of using the Fourth Gospel to decide whether, as a matter of history, Jesus made a personal claim to divinity as the Son of God must be abandoned. Though John certainly used items from the tradition of the sayings of Jesus, the major discourses in which such claims are made are more like the speeches in a play, in which the author expresses a considered understanding of the function and meaning of the characters. The Gospel of John is far too complex for a simplistic view of its historical value to be plausible.

Another false expectation arises from the philosophical and spiritual aspects of the Gospel. Some people wrongly suppose that John is a treatise on the life of prayer. It is true that those who wish to explore the ways of contemplative prayer will find much food for thought in John. Indeed, John's spirituality, expressed in terms of a mutual indwelling of God and Jesus and the disciples (14.18-24), is most valuable for those who read the Gospel with the aim of deepening their spiritual life. But it was not written as a guide to prayer. Its value for this purpose operates at a deeper level of apprehension of its message.

Finally, John is not a resource-book for dealing with moral questions. Good and evil are treated in terms of truth and falsehood, and sin is usually a matter of refusal to put faith in

Jesus. The only moral virtue is the love command (13.34-35; 15.1-17), but that does in a sense embrace all the others. But there is no extended treatment of moral issues in John.

The Jews in John

One particular matter must be settled at the outset, which affects the whole tone of the Gospel, and presents a difficult problem for many modern readers. This is the strange way in which the opponents of Jesus are constantly referred to simply as 'the Jews'. It is strange, because of course Jesus and his friends are Jews too. There are various ways of explaining this, but, whatever the reason, the effect has been extremely unfortunate. It lays John wide open to the charge of anti-Semitism. This is so undesirable in a sacred book, which is treasured as the revelation of the love of God for all people, that serious thought needs to be given to the question whether new translations should seek a way round this, just as the problem of sexist language has to be faced by modern translators. In both cases what is at stake is not the true meaning of the text, but the impact of a literal translation on a highly sensitive area of modern consciousness. One can get around it to some extent by substituting 'the Jerusalem authorities' for 'the Jews', as this is what is usually meant. But this is not sufficient to cope with the vicious tone of 8.31-47, in which the descendants of Abraham are referred to *en bloc* as sons of the devil. And of course Jesus is the speaker. We may well ask if Jesus spoke of his own people in this way. Was he an anti-Semitist? Some people would take the Gospel of John as evidence that he was.

Here, then, is an issue which demands patient and objective study on the part of every modern reader. It is not enough to try to remove the problem by means of a technicality, such as the suggestion that 'the Jews' means the inhabitants of the province of Judea in contrast with the Galileans. Nor can we distinguish between the ruling classes who opposed Jesus as 'the Jews', and the common people who accepted him, because the designation has the effect of fatally blurring this distinction.

On the other hand there is not the least reason to suppose that the evangelist wishes to encourage anti-Semitism. John's intentions are clarified by the somewhat bitter editorial observation in 12.42-43. The context shows that the real issue is the failure of the first Christians to convert the majority of their fellow-Jews. It was the cause of much pain and heart-searching among the earliest Christians, who wondered how it could be fitted into God's plan of salvation. An answer was found in the prophecy of Isa. 6.9-10, which tells of the disobedience of the people, who are deaf to God's message. This is quoted several times in the New Testament (cf. Matt. 13.14-15; Acts 28.26-27), and appears here in the present context in John 12.40. John's comment in 12.42 has been recognised, especially since the work of J.L. Martyn, as a retrojection of the situation in John's own time (perhaps 85-90 CE). By this time relations between Christians (especially Jewish Christians) and the majority of Jews had reached breaking point. There was mutual hostility, and it is not possible to exonerate either side. The subsequent history, when the Christians gained power, is a shaming story for Christians, and it is this subsequent experience which has defined the idea of anti-Semitism ever afterwards. John shows the beginning of this sad state of affairs, but the issue in the Gospel is not whether one is a Jew or not, but whether one is a believer. In fact 'the Jews' in John means 'the unbelieving Jews', no more and no less, and the application of this to the Jerusalem authorities reflects the situation referred to in 12.42-43.

Inclusive Language

John's presentation of Jesus has been deeply influenced by the tradition of Jesus' own spirituality, which is exemplified in the Lord's Prayer and is expressed in his characteristic address to God as *Abba,* which means Father. John not only retains this in prayers of Jesus (11.41; 12.27-28; 17.1, 5, 11, 25), but also makes extensive use of the correlation Father and Son in the discourses when Jesus is speaking of his relation to God throughout the Gospel. This feature of John is deeply meaningful and helpful to many readers, but it must be recognised that the use of specifically masculine concepts can also be hurtful and alienating.

Obviously the Gospel cannot be rewritten to remove the language of Father and Son without doing violence to its literary form. But readers who are sensitive to this issue may like to substitute in their own minds the correlation Parent and Offspring, or Parent and Child. This can be justified from the Prologue of the Gospel (1.1-18). Here John sets out the philosophical basis of the relationship between God and Jesus in terms of the incarnation of the Word of God. The use of Word (*logos*)to denote the coeternal Offspring of God replaces Wisdom in the literary models which lie behind the Prologue (Prov. 8.22-31; Ecclesiasticus 24; Wisd. 7.22-8.1). Wisdom (Hebrew *ḥokmah,* Greek *sophia*) is a feminine word, and so is often personified as a woman. John had to avoid this because of the incarnation of the Offspring in the man Jesus. At this point a parenthesis in v. 14 is important, though often misunderstood on account of faulty translation. 'The Word became flesh,' says John, 'and we saw his glory, *glory as of an only son of a father'.* This is an analogy, and the usual translation 'glory as of the only Son from the Father' (*RSV*) is incorrect. 'Glory' here virtually means 'reflection'. Thus Jesus reflects the glory of God as a son reflects the aspect of a father on account of family likeness, and of course that is true of parent and offspring without regard to sex. It is thus clear that the Father and Son language in John is always a matter of analogy. John knows that, when one passes from analogy to direct language about God, one passes to a realm of understanding where sexual differentiation is transcended.

Further Reading

The most useful general study of the Fourth Gospel for reference on the kind of issues which have been introduced in this chapter is S.S. Smalley, *John. Evangelist and Interpreter,* Exeter: Paternoster Press, 1978. A short introduction is provided by J. Painter, *John. Witness and Theologian,* London: SPCK, 1975. A survey of modern study of John is given by R. Kysar, *The Fourth Evangelist and his Gospel,* Minneapolis: Augsburg, 1975. He has brought it up to date in an article, 'The Gospel of John in Current Research', *Religious Studies Review* 9, 1983, pp. 314-23.

The essay of Wayne Meeks, 'The Man from Heaven in Johannine Sectarianism'. will be found in John Ashton, *The Interpretation of*

John, London: SPCK, 1986, pp. 147-73. This is a reprint of eight essays on various aspects of John by leading scholars which have had seminal importance in the twentieth century, some translated into English for the first time. Ashton's own 'Introduction' to this volume is a valuable summary of recent trends in the study of John. Also useful is David Rensberger, *Overcoming the World. Politics and Community in the Gospel of John,* London: SPCK, 1988, especially chapter 1, 'The New Era in Johannine Interpretation'.

2

THE EVANGELIST
AND THE GOSPEL

Who was the Author?

OUR STUDY OF THE QUESTION of the Jews in John has shown
that it is necessary to take into account conditions towards the
end of the first century, when the strained relations between
church and synagogue were near to disruption. This at once
indicates that, in spite of attempts to assign John to an earlier
date, a date fairly late in the century is required. This does not
conflict with the traditional date for John, because that was
always put in the nineties, even though the evangelist was
identified with the apostle John and regarded as an eye-
witness of what is recorded in the Gospel. Assuming that the
apostle is also to be identified with the 'elder' of the Johannine
Epistles (2 John 1; 3 John 1), an appealing picture can be
gained of the evangelist as a very old man, who addresses his
readers as 'little children' (e.g. 1 John 2.1). This picture
remains the most widely accepted popular opinion concerning
the authorship of the Fourth Gospel.

However, it is already clear that the Gospel of John is far too
complex to be considered merely an old man's reminiscences.
If the late date is accepted, the length of time available allows
for the formation and reworking of traditions over a long
period before the actual writing of the Gospel. One possibility is
that the apostle John was the *originator* of the special
traditions which lie behind the Fourth Gospel, and these were
preserved and developed in the Johannine church until
someone else wove them into the finished form of the Gospel.

The important point here is not whether the apostle John
was the originator of the special traditions, but the fact that,

whatever their provenance, it is the evangelist who comes at the *end* of the process who is the real author of the Fourth Gospel. This person may have had access to some accurate traditions, derived from an eye-witness, but the Gospel shows that it was never intended to be a simple historical account of the life of Jesus, as we have already seen.

Of course it does have to be recognised that John constantly makes claims concerning the truth, but this refers to the message, not to a special source of information. On the other hand there is a definite statement about authorship in the Appendix (21.24), which cannot be simply brushed aside. We shall therefore look carefully at the evidence about authorship before considering the way in which the task of writing the Gospel has been approached. This will introduce the factors which have gone into the making of the Gospel, in which the relationship between the underlying tradition and the creative handling of it by the evangelist can be put into perspective.

John

We start from the fact that the Fourth Gospel has always been known as the Gospel according to John, and this goes with the traditional view that the evangelist was the apostle John. Although this tradition continues to have supporters among modern scholars, the majority cling to it only in the most tenuous form, or abandon it altogether. It is thus important to see the reasons why the traditional identification is regarded by most scholars as untenable.

The name John does not actually occur in reference to an apostle in the Gospel at all. In 1.37-40 we hear of an unnamed disciple. But even if he is identified with the evangelist, as some have supposed, it is unlikely that John son of Zebedee is intended, because the context makes no room for his brother James. In the Appendix (21.2) the two sons of Zebedee are mentioned in a group of seven disciples, but they are not named individually. But two others of the seven are not named at all, so there are really four disciples with whom the writer might be identified, and it is arbitrary to decide that he is John. The matter is complicated further by the fact that one of these four is referred to in v. 7 as 'the disciple whom Jesus loved'. The Beloved Disciple has already appeared at 13.23; 19.26; 20.2, and although he is traditionally identified with John, in fact his identity is never disclosed. It seems, then, that the author is deliberately hiding the identity of the Beloved Disciple, and it must be judged unlikely that one of the sons of Zebedee is meant in 21.2 rather than one of those left unnamed.

The strongest external evidence in favour of the identification with John is the statement of Clement of Alexandria, preserved in Eusebius (*H. E.* 6.14.7), written about 180 CE. 'Last of all John, perceiving that the external facts had been made plain in the Gospels, being urged by his friends and inspired by the Spirit, composed a spiritual gospel.' But we know from Irenaeus (*Adv. Haer.* 1.8.5) that the Gnostic Ptolemaeus had before this already composed a commentary on the Prologue of the Gospel, which he attributed to 'John, the disciple of the Lord'. Thus the Beloved Disciple is assumed (on the strength of 21.24) to be the author of the Gospel, and he has already been identified with the apostle John. The reason for this identification in the middle of the second century is obvious. By this time apostolic authorship was becoming an essential criterion for acceptance. We should also note that in the quotation from Clement above, Clement is concerned to explain the *late* appearance of the Fourth Gospel, which did not become widely known until long after the general diffusion of the Synoptic Gospels. So the conditions were laid down for the long-standing tradition that the Gospel was written by an apostle some sixty years after the events which it describes, thus making an exceptional combination of a late date and a claim to eye-witness reporting. But the identification of this person with the apostle John may well have arisen simply as a means of claiming apostolic authorship for a work that was actually anonymous.

For this reason it is really a mistake to look for *other* people called John who might have written the Gospel, or for that matter to look for anyone else in the New Testament, though numerous suggestions have been proposed along these lines. What is more important is to decide whether the editorial note in 21.24 is correct in identifying the evangelist with the Beloved Disciple. This at least might save the claim to eye-witness testimony, even if the evangelist's name has been lost beyond recall.

The Beloved Disciple

Doubt about the identity of the Beloved Disciple does not automatically exclude the view that he was a real person, actually present on the occasions where he is mentioned (13.23; 19.26; 20.2; 21.7, 20-23; possibly also 1.35; 18.15; 19.35). But apart from the editorial note in 21.24, there is no indication in the text that he was the author of the Gospel as we know it. Many scholars today dismiss 21.24 as a false deduction. Manifestly the purpose of the note is to legitimate the Gospel, and this ties up with its late diffusion and difficulty in gaining acceptance in orthodox Christian circles.

However, the information in 21.24 can be accepted as broadly true if the Beloved Disciple is identified with the founder of the Johannine tradition. Though Bultmann denied that the Beloved Disciple was ever intended to be more than a fictitious, ideal figure, in the last forty years there has been a growing critical consensus that he is a real historical person, whose testimony lies behind the Fourth Gospel. On this view full weight is given to the fact that the Gospel shows signs of being the end-product of a long literary process, in which the core information has been worked up by successive hands, forming a distinctive 'Johannine school'. If this is correct, it can be reasonably claimed that the Beloved Disciple is the source of the special information in the Gospel and the inspiration of the 'school' of which he was the founder.

The Beloved Disciple on this view constitutes a precious link between the actual history of Jesus and the formation of the Gospel. But he is not responsible for its final form and cannot be identified with the evangelist. This leaves open the question of eye-witness reporting, for the extent to which that has survived in the final form is impossible to determine.

In spite of this growing consensus, I find myself siding with Bultmann on this issue on literary grounds. To me the Beloved Disciple is a creation of the evangelist in order to serve a specific function. He is one of the Twelve, who at crucial moments gives expression to the evangelist's own views. He represents true discipleship, understanding the necessity of the death of Jesus when all others fail. He is thus a foil to Peter, who in spite of being the acknowledged leader failed by denying Jesus three times. Thus the Beloved Disciple is in one sense the evangelist, because he embodies the evangelist's own faith. But in another sense he is one with whom the *reader* should identify, for the whole purpose of the Gospel is to convey the same understanding to every reader. Once we see the function of the Beloved Disciple in this way, a new dimension opens up in the study of John, the literary dimension of rhetorical effect and reader-response, which is just as important for understanding the Gospel as the question of its historical value.

On this view the Beloved Disciple is an ambiguous and intriguing personality, and it would not be surprising if the Johannine church thought he must be the evangelist making a veiled self-reference. One purpose of the appendix (21.1-23) might be to deal with this suggestion. If so, v. 23 refuses to divulge his identity and throws it back to the readers to look to their own discipleship. For of course the Beloved Disciple is *both* the evangelist *and* the readers from a functional point of view. However, it seems that some still thought that he was literally the evangelist, and this idea is embodied in the editorial note of v. 24, and in the end prevailed.

The Function of the Beloved Disciple

When we turn to the actual passages in which the Beloved Disciple is mentioned, we are at once faced with the problem of John's use of historical tradition.

First we note that John does not mention any of the three occasions when the sons of Zebedee and Peter were taken aside by Jesus according to the Synoptic tradition (cf. Mark 5.37; 9.2; 14.33). This would be extraordinary if the Beloved Disciple were really John the apostle. The Beloved Disciple, however, is first marked out in John's account of the Last Supper (13.21-30). This is a passage which clearly has a close relation to the Synoptic tradition. In the Synoptics Jesus prophesies that one of the disciples will betray him (Matt. 26.21 = Mark 14.18). John reproduces almost exactly the

same words as Mark (13.21). Mark gives no indication who
the traitor might be in spite of recording the anxious
questioning of the Twelve. Matthew, however, changes this to
a question by Judas alone, who thereby incriminates himself.
In John this feature is built up in a highly dramatic way. The
questioning becomes a signal by Peter to the Beloved Disciple
to find out, as he is close to the breast of Jesus. So the Beloved
Disciple alone is privileged to understand what Jesus is doing.

It is clear that in this brilliant presentation of the tradition,
which is remarkable for its dramatic irony, John is writing for
the benefit of the readers. The aim is to teach the true
meaning of discipleship. The Beloved Disciple is present, close
to Jesus, but there is only the briefest whispered conversation,
and otherwise he is a silent spectator. Unlike Peter, he does not
loudly assert his willingness to follow Jesus to death—but
neither does he deny him three times. Thus the function of the
Beloved Disciple is only to express understanding of Jesus, and
that is what the evangelist hopes to achieve in the readers.

This functional purpose of the character of the Beloved
Disciple favours the suggestion that John has added him into
the story of the Last Supper, which is based on older traditions
which made no mention of him. The same thing happens in
the second episode (19.25-27), where the mother of Jesus is
assumed to be one of the women at the cross (cf. Matt. 27.56;
Mark 15.40) and the Beloved Disciple, who actually becomes
her new son, is a newcomer to the tradition. The Beloved
Disciple enters the story again in 20.2-10, when he runs with
Peter to see the empty tomb. It is he who draws the correct
conclusion from what they see, and believes in the
resurrection. As before, there is a Synoptic parallel, in which
the Beloved Disciple does not figure at all. This is Luke 24.12,
which is unfamiliar to many modern readers because it has
been banished to the footnotes in several modern translations
(e.g. RSV, NEB, REB) on text-critical grounds. But even if it is
not original in Luke, it is still likely to be a tradition about Peter
which did not include the Beloved Disciple, rather than a gloss
derived from John.

Finally the Beloved Disciple features once more in the
Appendix, 21.1-23. The basic story is the miraculous catch of
fish, which again has a parallel in Luke, but in connection

with the original call of the first disciples (Luke 5.1-11). In John 21 the motif of discipleship is also the chief issue. As we have seen, John (like Luke) mentions Peter and the sons of Zebedee, but it is probable that the Beloved Disciple is one of two others left unnamed, so that his identity is not disclosed. Once more he functions as one who can recognise the risen Lord without full physical sight (vv. 4, 7). The final point in the story is that, whereas Peter is reinstated as a disciple of Jesus (vv. 15-17), even to the extent of matching his death (vv. 18-19, cf. 13.37), the Beloved Disciple will continue to follow Jesus until he comes again—precisely because he is the model for every reader (vv. 20-23).

Fact and Fiction in John

By suggesting that the Beloved Disciple has been added into the underlying source on each occasion when he appears, we have opened up the whole question of the relationship between fact and fiction in John. To many people these are mutually exclusive alternatives. Either John's life of Jesus is historical, and should be accepted as it stands, or it is fictitious, and therefore a worthless forgery. Modern scholarship of all shades of opinion seeks to find a middle way between these two extremes. Some scholars veer to the side of fact, others to the side of considerable creativity on the part of the evangelist. But even on a maximalist view of historicity, room must be left for some degree of author's licence. John uses a highly dramatic style of presentation. The treatment of the theme of questioning about the traitor in 13.21-30 is perhaps the most stunning example. A historical play, like Shakespeare's *Richard II*, is not judged to be true or false by its accuracy of detail, which cannot possibly be reproduced on the stage, but by its success in conveying the real issues and the character of the leading personalities. It must also be pointed out that the Synoptic writers also use author's licence in their own ways. Where Matthew and Mark overlap, either Matthew has drastically reduced Mark or Mark has expanded Matthew (cf. Matt. 8.28-34 = Mark 5.1-20, where Mark is more than twice the length of Matthew). John is therefore not alone in exercising freedom in writing up the gospel traditions. But

John's aims are more complex and the method involves a greater degree of creativity.

If the evangelist was not an eye-witness of the events, dependence on sources was inescapable. These were not plentiful, and suffered distortion with the passage of time. John did not have a private pipe-line of authentic tradition, but had to use the same kind of sources as the Synoptic writers. These must be understood before we can go further in assessing the special quality of the Gospel of John.

Sources for the Life of Jesus

All four Gospels should be regarded primarily as biographies of Jesus, but all four have a definite theological aim. The modern approach to biography was unknown in the ancient world, and the evangelists' concept of their task is quite similar to Suetonius' *Lives of the Caesars*. To take Mark as an example, there is a clear theological aim, which corresponds with the primitive preaching. Jesus proclaimed the kingdom of God, was crucified, and was raised by God to be exalted as the Messiah of the coming kingdom. So Mark shows Jesus preaching the kingdom, and eventually crucified, and the Gospel ends with the announcement of the resurrection (Mark 16.1-8). At the same time the theme of Jesus' identity runs through Mark, reaching a minor climax with Peter's confession at Caesarea Philippi half-way through the Gospel (Mark 8.27-30), and a final climax with the confession of the centurion immediately after Jesus' death on the cross (Mark 15.39). In fact this theological structure of Mark has a certain similarity to that of John.

Mark achieved his aim mainly by the arrangement of material and editorial linkages, but without radical rewriting of the sources. These were largely anecdotes, and there are signs that some of them had already been put together in short collections, e.g. Mark 2.1–3.6; 4.1-34. Similarly it is widely held that Matthew and Luke made use of a collection of the teachings of Jesus (the so-called Q document). But such collections do not amount to strictly historical records. By the time that the Gospels were written the materials for a proper life of Jesus did not exist. No contemporary records were kept, and no one thought about writing a life of him until it was almost too late. For the most part Mark had to make do with an assortment of traditions, consisting of memories of Jesus which had been repeated orally without any control of accuracy before being committed to writing. Form-critical study of these traditions has shown that they owe their survival to their practical use in the community for the instruction of new members and similar purposes. Thus these traditions were repeated because of their social function, but this would be likely to lead to some degree of distortion to make them relevant.

Nevertheless it would be absurd to claim that the truth about Jesus was totally lost in this process. The anecdotes and collected sayings of Jesus crystallize the impression of him and his message as he was remembered. What we have in the Synoptic Gospels is three 'identikit' portraits of Jesus, each differing to some extent on account of the outlook of the evangelist, but all recognisably the same person, even though none is a photograph taken from life.

John's picture of Jesus, however, is different. This could be due to the use of independent traditions, not known to the other evangelists, but it might also be due to far greater use of author's licence, resulting in a more individual portrait, possibly further removed from historical accuracy. Which is it likely to be?

John and the Synoptic Tradition

To answer this question we must look at the extent to which John and the Synoptics are in agreement. First, we can distinguish between anecdotes and discourses. The anecdotes (e.g. healing miracles) are usually very similar to the Synoptic material, even though they may have important variations in detail. The discourses, on the other hand, are entirely different. They are reasoned arguments on such subjects as the divine authority of Jesus himself, quite unlike the Synoptic sermons of Jesus (Matthew 5–7; Luke 6), his tirade against the scribes and Pharisees (Matthew 23) or the apocalyptic discourse (Mark 13). The difference can be seen very clearly in John 5. Here a Synoptic-type healing story (vv. 1-9, including an almost identical verbal parallel with Mark 2.11 in v. 8), is followed by a dialogue with the Jerusalem authorities (vv. 10-18). This prepares the ground for a long monologue of Jesus on his authority, which has no Synoptic links (vv. 19-47).

Secondly, there are sayings of Jesus in a proverbial style which have close parallels in the Synoptic tradition. Some of these are put together in short sequences (notably 4.35-38; 12.24-26; 13.16-20). Others are scattered through the discourses (e.g. 3.3, 5; 8.51), often with the opening 'Amen, amen, I say to you', as in the Synoptic Gospels (e.g. Matt. 18.3, which may be an independent version of the saying in John 3.3, 5).

Thirdly, John's passion narrative (chapters 18–19) has a general resemblance to the Synoptic passion narratives, in spite of many differences of detail.

Various theories have been proposed to account for these similarities and differences. It can be argued that John is directly dependent on one or more of the Synoptic Gospels in the places where there is close verbal agreement. But it is never a simple relationship. For instance, John's account of the Feeding of the Multitude is followed by the Walking on Water (6.1-21), as in Mark 6.32-52, and there are many features in common with Mark. But some details of vocabulary are closer to the parallel narrative in Matthew. Also there are links with the second feeding in Mark 8.1-10 and with other sea episodes, such as Mark 4.35-41. Thus it is not just a matter of following one of the Synoptic accounts. It could be the case that John had a general familiarity with all the Synoptic accounts, which became merged in the retelling. There must be many preachers who have done this.

An alternative view, which has been gaining ground in recent study, is based on the assumption that many traditions about Jesus were transmitted through more than one channel. This can indeed be seen within Mark, for the two feeding miracles in Mark 6 and 8 are surely variant versions of the same event. The advantage of this view is that it explains why John's use of traditions parallel to the Synoptic Gospels is so patchy, and it also accounts for further material of similar type (e.g. the Marriage at Cana, 2.1-10).

In the passion narrative (John 18–19) and some of the events leading up to it (11.47–12.17) it is possible to trace a closer connection with Mark, but this may be due to the fact that the main outline of the passion narrative was relatively fixed before it was reproduced by Mark, because it was retold each year in the Christian Passover. Moreover there are features in John which have close links with the special material in Luke. Here again opinion is divided whether John used Luke or had access to Luke's source. A glimpse at one of these passages will show the complexity of the relationship between John and the Synoptics and the difficulty of reaching a definitive conclusion.

John and the Anointing of Jesus

The story of the Raising of Lazarus (11.1-44) is set in the household of Mary and Martha at Bethany, very near to Jerusalem. Then in 12.1-8 their home is the place where Jesus is anointed by a woman during a meal. This corresponds with Mark 14.3-9, but there the house is the home of Simon the leper, and the woman is not named. Here, however, Mary attends to Jesus while Martha serves the meal, just as in the entirely separate story of the two sisters in Luke 10.38-42, which is set in an unnamed village, presumably in Galilee, long before Jesus goes up to Jerusalem. Moreover, whereas the woman in Mark anoints Jesus' head, Mary in John anoints his feet, and wipes them with her hair. This links up with another Galilean episode, Luke 7.36-50, in which a Pharisee entertains Jesus to a meal, and an unnamed woman washes his feet with her tears and wipes them with her hair, before anointing them as an additional act. This woman is traditionally identified with Mary Magdalene (mentioned two verses later in Luke 8.2), but John does not seem to be aware of this, in spite of naming her Mary.

How are these links to be explained? In my view, the simplest solution is that John's basis was the Bethany story as it is found in Mark 14.3-9. This was already associated with the passion narrative in the tradition because of the reference to the burial of Jesus (Mark 14.8, cf. John 12.7). But John took the *setting* from the story of Martha and Mary, with the detail that 'Martha served' (cf. Luke 10.40). Also the anointing of the *feet* of Jesus and wiping with hair reflect the other story in Luke (using the same words as Luke 7.38). But these connections become simpler when we observe that Luke's *source* at Luke 7.38 probably did not include anointing at all, but simply had washing the feet with tears and wiping with hair. Luke has added in the motif of anointing from the Bethany story, which he omits from the passion narrative, though it is clear that he knows that anointing should apply to the head rather than the feet (Luke 7.46). If, then, John was dependent on Luke's source rather than Luke as such, the way was open to *substitute* the anointing of the feet of Jesus instead of washing them. Thus John uses the Bethany story, but takes the motif of the feet from Luke's source, whereas Luke reproduces the source, but adds into it the motif of anointing from the Bethany story. Moreover, if John had the story in an independent source, it is likely that it contained the other story of Mary and Martha in close proximity to it. This explains how John has been able to use this as the setting, and also why John does not make the identification with Mary Magdalene, because the source did not contain Luke 8.1-3.

Before we leave this example, we must ask why John chose to take the one detail of the feet from the Galilean story. When we compare John's anointing story with the account of the Last Supper in chapter 13, it at once becomes apparent that there are subtle links between them, which prepare the reader for the issues at stake. The apparently pointless detail that 'Martha served' now falls into place. It prepares for Jesus' teaching on service in 13.12-17. Similarly Mary's washing of Jesus' feet with ointment prepares for Jesus' washing of the disciples' feet in vv. 4-11. Moreover the reference to Jesus' burial relates the tradition to his death. Jesus' washing of the disciples' feet is an act of service which signifies cleansing in a deeper sense, the total cleansing which is effected by the saving death of Jesus and appropriated in baptism (briefly and allusively indicated in Jesus' answer to Peter in 13.10).

One more dramatic link is provided by the disciples' complaint that the expensive ointment should have been sold for the poor. In John it is Judas who makes this complaint, and the point is underlined with the information (not known from any other source) that Judas was the treasurer and used to pilfer the common fund (12.4-6). This information is taken up and used with great skill in 13.28-29. Here the disciples think that Judas' departure from the Supper is to give money to the poor. In fact it is, as only the Beloved Disciple (and the reader!) knows, to betray Jesus to death.

John's Use of Sources

The example of the anointing story has illustrated several features of John's use of sources, even if we cannot be certain whether it is based on the Synoptic Gospels as we know them or on the kind of sources underlying them. First, it shows that sources of this type certainly lie behind the Fourth Gospel. Secondly, the use of elements drawn from several different stories to make a composite picture can be observed elsewhere, and must be regarded as a feature of John's compositional technique. Thus the healing of a paralysed man at the pool of Bethesda (or Beth-zatha) in 5.1-9 also seems to have three components. a Jerusalem healing story in 5.1-7, unknown from the Synoptic tradition; the conclusion in v. 8, expressed in words from the famous story of the man let down through the roof of a house in Capernaum (Mark 2.11); an additional note in v. 9 that this was done on the sabbath, introduced for the sake of the dialogue in vv. 10-18.

A third feature of John's use of sources is the freedom exercised in adapting them. This may seem reprehensible at first sight, but a little thought shows that it is inevitable. John's methods are no worse than what we find in Matthew, where the man with a legion in Mark 5.1-20 has become *two* men in Matt. 8.28-34. This sort of thing falls within the bounds of an author's licence.

Fourthly, the subtle relationship between the anointing story and John's Last Supper account shows the care and deliberation of the evangelist. The irony of the presentation is intended to make the reader think of the deeper issues—in this case the meaning of discipleship in the light of the sacrificial death of Jesus, which is set off by the contrast of Judas. Hence full recognition must be accorded to the evangelist as a creative writer, who should not be dissolved into a mass of hands in a 'school' which produced the Fourth Gospel over a long period. Previous layers of the Johannine tradition are either sources comparable to those which lie behind the Synoptic Gospels, or earlier workings of the evangelist, in which these features of style were developed and perfected.

The Signs Source

In his great commentary on John, Bultmann took up the suggestion of Faure that the miracle stories in John were drawn from a special source, which can be referred to as the Signs Source. The numbering of the first two signs (2.11 and 4.54) seemed to support this theory, though both verses contain obviously Johannine elements. Basically the suggestion is harmless enough, as such a collection is comparable to the series in Mark 2.1–3.6. But Bultmann sought to prove that the source had a distinct theological tendency to which the evangelist was opposed, in spite of making use of the source almost intact. This was a popular presentation of Jesus as a miracle-worker, developed in a Hellenistic milieu to make him out to be a divinity. In a Hellenistic setting, where popular pagan religion was influenced by Greek ideas, such a person would be regarded as a *theios anēr* (divine man), i.e. one in whom divine powers were at work, who might be raised to the company of the gods at his death, or he might even be considered to be one of the gods visiting the world in human likeness (cf. Acts 13.11). In John it was claimed that a distinction could be made between *sēmeia* = 'signs', identified with the miracles interpreted in the light of this unsatisfactory christology, and *erga* = 'works', identified with the miracles understood as the saving acts of God. Thus the people tend to evince an inadequate faith in Jesus in response to his signs (cf. 2.22; 3.2), but Jesus challenges them to perceive them as the 'works ' of God in order to reach genuine faith (e.g. 5.20; 10.37-38). This theory was elaborated by Fortna (1970), who attempted to reconstruct a 'Signs Gospel', including a passion narrative, as the major narrative source behind the Fourth Gospel.

This theory is open to several objections. In the first place, the semi-pagan christology attributed to the source is unknown in the New Testament. It is really most improbable that the evangelist would engage in polemic with the source at the same time as reproducing it almost word for word. In fact this impression is really a feature of John's dialogue technique, whereby a person is made to misunderstand an initial statement of Jesus in order to evoke a further definition at a deeper level of meaning. The classic examples are Nicodemus in 3.4, 9 and the Samaritan woman in 4.11, 15. Examples involving miracles are the dialogues of chapters 5 and 9. Fortna, in a recent revision of his work (1989), has abandoned the idea of a 'divine man' christology. In his view the source had an orthodox doctrine of Jesus as the Messiah, but it was simplistic and needed to be greatly elaborated to serve the evangelist's purpose.

Secondly, the word *sēmeion* cannot be used as a source criterion. It occurs more frequently in John's editorial writing than in the material attributed to the source, and it does not carry a pejorative sense, so that the contrast with *ergon* cannot be maintained. The *signs* are intended to produce faith (20.30-31) so that the people may accept Jesus as the one who does the *works* of God which are the eschatological acts of salvation (5.20-23).

Thirdly, the attempt to reconstruct the source out of the text of the Gospel grievously underestimates the extent of John's reworking of sources, and fails to establish convincing criteria for deciding what belongs to the source. Even though John may not have made direct use of the Synoptic Gospels, the proper starting-point for source analysis must always be the passages which have parallels with them, where John's handling of such traditions can be most easily seen.

The Discourse Source

The discourses of John, on the other hand, present a sharp contrast with all the known sources for the life of Jesus, and thus require a different explanation. Here again Bultmann proposed a Revelation-Discourse Source. In this case his

proposal was far more radical, for he argued that it was the
work of a proto-Gnostic sect, adapted to apply to Jesus.

As the name implies, the source was held to be a collection of
revelations given by a Revealer from heaven. These conveyed
the secret knowledge (*gnōsis*) whereby mortal human beings
could be freed from the imprisonment of earthly existence and
ascend in spirit to the divine life, following the ascent of the
Revealer himself. This 'Saviour-myth' belonged to the
teaching of a pre-Christian Gnostic sect, which Bultmann
identified with the ancient sect of the Mandaeans, still
surviving in Iran. Their system is based on a radical dualism,
the aim being to escape from the realm of darkness into the
divine light. Their religious titles preserve the Aramaic
language of their origins, and so point to Syria as their first
home. The writings of the sect show hostility to Jesus, but give
honour to John the Baptist, who is identified with the heavenly
deliverer (Enosh-Uthra). It remains uncertain, however,
whether the Baptist is an original feature. But Bultmann saw
this as the key to the connection with Christian origins (for the
Baptist sect cf. Acts 18.25; 19.1-7). Thus John took over a
Gnostic document, in which the Baptist was the Revealer, and
applied it to Jesus. The document was composed in Semitic
poetic style comparable to the Wisdom literature. This can be
seen in the Prologue and in numerous discourse passages
elsewhere (e.g. 3.31-36).

For the subject-matter of the document Bultmann
compared the non-canonical *Odes of Solomon,* which are
second-century poems on themes of divine truth, which
survive in a Syriac version. But they are not necessarily the
product of a Gnostic sect, and the similarities with John are
more likely to be due to dependence on John than the other
way round. However, the more recent discovery of Gnostic
writings from Nag Hammadi has provided much better
models, and shows that a document of the kind proposed by
Bultmann is by no means impossible.

Nevertheless, the Johannine discourses are not primarily
concerned with this kind of spirituality, but with presenting
Jesus in person as the object of faith. This was recognised by
Bultmann, who argued that John radically altered the
character of the document, just as in the case of the Signs

Source. The alteration here consisted in making the secret knowledge the revelation of the identity of Jesus himself. Those who believe in Jesus are enabled to enjoy eternal life. They thus already possess the future benefits which belong to the coming age in the thought of earliest Christianity. Thus the source, with its timeless and mystical concept of salvation, enabled John to break through the eschatological frame of the primitive kerygma (proclamation), producing a 'realised eschatology', i.e. the idea of present realisation of what properly belongs to the future (cf. 5.25). At the time when the Gospel was written the delay of the parousia, or second coming, of Jesus was causing a crisis of confidence in the church's message. John's discourses supply the necessary reinterpretation of the message to show its permanent value, regardless of the passage of time. In adapting the source the evangelist was careful to retain the centrality of the preaching of the cross in the kerygma (which of course the source did not contain), so that the necessity of the death of Jesus is presented as an essential aspect of the meaning of faith in him (cf. 3.14-16; 8.28-29).

As before, it must be questioned whether a source of this kind is a necessary hypothesis. In any case, the source cannot be separated out from the rest of the Gospel on grounds of style. The very considerable adaptation which would be required to make such a source suitable for John's purpose suggests that a better explanation would be to regard the postulated document not as a source but as a model.

But if it is models that we are looking for, there are other possibilities which are nearer to the beginnings of Christianity in a Jewish setting. The Prologue is most likely to be modelled on Jewish Wisdom poems, as we have seen. Again, the discourse on the Bread of Life in 6.32-58 is based on the Old Testament story of the manna in the wilderness in Exodus 16, and John expressly attributes it to teaching given by Jesus in the synagogue at Capernaum (6.59). This suggests that the model is the synagogue homily or sermon, in which the liturgical lessons or Scripture readings are expounded, such as we find in the Jewish *midrash*. As it is only the Prologue which appears to have literary models behind it, it is reasonable to suppose that the rest of the discourses are based on the evangelist's own homilies delivered in the Johannine church.

The Homilies of John

The observation that the discourses of John are modelled on homilies brings them back into the mainstream of Christian life, and so makes them seem less strange as the work of the evangelist. Moreover this theory greatly eases the problem of understanding the relationship between the discourses. For, in spite of some cross-referencing, the discourses tend to be complete in themselves. This view has been espoused by a number of modern commentators, notably R.E. Brown. He argues that the homilies stem from the work of the Beloved Disciple (assumed to be the founder of the Johannine tradition), which was taken up and used by the evangelist. But in my opinion it is a mistake to distinguish between the author of the homilies and the evangelist. It is much better to think of the homilies as the evangelist's own preaching, in which the technique was worked out. On this view the homilies are best regarded as the evangelist's first drafts, incorporated with varying degrees of alteration into the larger work.

The homiletic theory thus explains the unique feature of the discourses, but we still have to ask what sources were available for them in the first place. Here the analogy of a modern preacher may help. A preacher may start from a passage of scripture, taking a text from it as the opening of the sermon, and then build up the sermon as an exposition and application of it. John does not begin with a passage of the Hebrew Scriptures, but with an item from the tradition of the sayings of Jesus. A glance at the opening verses of the discourses will show that a saying from the tradition is the starting-point far more than is commonly realised.

Some of the discourses begin with a narrative from the tradition (e.g. 5.1-9; 6.1-21), which serves the same purpose as a passage from Scripture. When this happens, John inserts dialogue to make the transition to the discourse (cf. 5.10-18; 6.22-30). But the discourse itself, based on a homily, has its own saying from the tradition, which we can regard as the text of the sermon. Thus the discourse with Nicodemus starts with a saying (3.3, 5), which has already been shown to be a traditional saying of Jesus (cf. Matt. 18.3; Mark 10.15). It provides the motif of origination from God, which is the theme of the whole discourse (cf. vv. 6, 31). Similarly in 5.19 Dodd detected a parable from the tradition, which he called the Parable of the Apprenticed Son. This opens up the theme of the authority of Jesus, who does 'nothing on my own authority' (v. 30). In the Bread of Life discourse Jesus' opening treatment of the topic in 6.32-34 contains a reminiscence of the Lord's Prayer (the response of the people in v. 34 echoes 'Give us this day our daily bread'). In 8.12 'I am the light of the world' has a Synoptic counterpart in Matt. 5.14, and introduces the theme of witness. In 8.31-38 a new discourse begins with a dialogue which includes another parable detected by Dodd, the Slave and the Son in v. 36. The Good Shepherd allegory of 10.7-18 is similarly based on the Parable of Sheep and Shepherd in 10.1-5.

Other sayings from the tradition occur at strategic points in the discourses, notably the eucharistic words of Jesus (cf. Mark 14.22-25) in 6.52-56 and a version of Mark 9.1 in 8.51, 52. Though they have been adapted for their present context in every case, they are sufficiently close to sayings which have survived in the Synoptic tradition to be recognised as source material.

If each discourse is basically a sermon expounding a text, we should not expect the main body of it to be derived from a source, as Bultmann supposed. It is altogether probable that it is the evangelist's own composition. John works like a playwright, who invents dialogue and speeches to convey the message of the play through the medium of drama. There is risk in this procedure, because it blurs the distinction between history and interpretation. Moreover, John's method seems to be a step on the way to what happened in the second century, when Gnostic teachers used the device of secret teaching by the risen Jesus as a vehicle for their own views. The justification of this procedure in John's case is the integrity with which the fundamental issues of Christian faith are exposed.

The Making of the Gospel

If the raw materials of the Gospel consisted of existing homilies and an assortment of other items from the tradition, it is not difficult to imagine the evangelist at work in making them into a coherent whole. It therefore comes as something of a surprise to find that there are various abrupt changes of theme and contradictions of time and place, which suggest a more complex process. Various suggestions have been made.

Bultmann's view, as we have seen, takes the Gospel to be based on three major sources, signs, discourses and passion narrative. He also postulated that the discourses had been disarranged through accidental displacement of sheets of the autograph. In his view a later editor, whom he called the Ecclesiastical Redactor, reassembled them in the wrong order, and at the same time showed his real aim of making John's teaching conform more closely with Christian orthodoxy by inserting various corrections. By these insertions he countered the timelessness of the teaching by bringing in references to the coming judgment in a literal way (e.g. 5.25-29). He also added allusions to the sacraments ('water' in 3.5 to make an allusion to baptism, and the eucharist in 6.51b-58), which the evangelist, having a wholly spiritual theology, would have disapproved. It must be said that most scholars find these suggestions arbitrary and unconvincing.

Brown, supporting the homiletic view, thought of the evangelist's work as the making of a consistent narrative on the basis of homilies, but accounted for the breaks of continuity by assuming that a later editor inserted further material which the evangelist had omitted. This explains some degree of overlap, e.g. 3.31-36 can be regarded as an alternative version of 3.16-21, and 6.51-58 repeats the substance of 6.35-50.

The possibility that the Gospel has been supplemented after the completion of the main composition should be accepted, because it gives the best explanation of some glaring difficulties. It is, in fact, almost universally recognised that chapter 21 has been added by a later editor after the original conclusion in 20.30-31, presumably after the death of the evangelist.

But it is also possible that the evangelist had already supplemented the Gospel with additional material, so as to incorporate further homiles which would reinforce the value of it. This theory solves several difficulties. One obvious example is chapter 6 on the Bread of Life. This is a self-contained piece, but it breaks the continuity between chapters 5 and 7, so that many commentators have argued that the chapter is misplaced and ought to follow chapter 4. But reasons can be found to suggest that it was deliberately placed after chapter 5. For instance, seeing that the Bread of Life discourse is based on the manna story in Exodus 16, it makes a superb example of the claim of Jesus in 5.46 that Moses 'wrote of me'. As interpolation is a more natural editorial procedure than accidental displacement, which is really quite hard to visualise, the theory that chapter 6 has been added in a second edition of the Gospel is worth serious consideration. Similarly the ending of 14.31, 'Rise, let us go hence', should obviously be followed by the walk to Gethsemane, but this does not happen until 18.1. Chapters 15 and 16, which go over some of the same themes as chapter 14, and the Prayer of Jesus in chapter 17 evince anxiety for the future safety of the disciples and the unity of the community, and so could be additional pieces in the light of new dangers.

Other possible changes in the second edition are the addition of the Prologue (1.1-18), which has had the original opening of the Gospel about the Baptist dovetailed into it (1.6-8), and the insertion of the Raising of Lazarus (11.1-44), which has replaced the Cleansing of the Temple (now moved to 2.13-22) as the immediate cause of the plot to arrest Jesus in 11.47-53 (cf. Mark 11.15-18). These changes have a theological interest. The Prologue provides the rational basis of the christology of John, which is presupposed throughout the Gospel, and (if it is indeed an addition for the second edition) was added precisely to clarify this. The Raising of Lazarus is a superbly dramatic presentation of Jesus as the lord of life and death before the account of his own death and resurrection in the narrative which follows.

The Woman taken in Adultery (7.53–8.11), which is an excerpt from a lost gospel, came into the text of John as late as the third century, and is not found in the best manuscripts.

The Style of John

One reason for insisting on the decisive role of the evangelist as the real author of the Gospel, including material introduced in a second edition, is the homogeneous style and vocabulary. This cuts across the division of sources proposed by Bultmann. A large number of typical features are present in all three divisions. Some of these are less frequent in material of Synoptic type (the signs and the passion narrative), and this encouraged Fortna to reconstruct his Signs Gospel out of this material. But this is a mistake, because specifically non-Johannine features are never sufficient to make possible reconstruction of the source in anything but the most fragmentary form.

The only way to appreciate John's style is to read the Gospel attentively, preferably in the original Greek. John's Greek is simple and straightforward. Because of its repetitiveness it is easy for beginners to grasp. Contrary to expectation, John does not use long philosophical words. Verbs are preferred to abstract nouns. The readers are constantly summoned to 'believe into' (*pisteuein eis*) Jesus, which means to entrust themselves to him, but the word for 'faith' (*pistis*) never occurs at all. Synonyms are used without discrimination (notably *pempein* and *apostellein* 'to send' and *agapān* and *philein* 'to love'). It is thus possible that Greek was not John's first language, which might well have been Aramaic if the Gospel originated in Syria.

However, these features are not enough to guarantee a single author, for there seems to be a common style in the writings of the Johannine community. The three Epistles of John are not necessarily the work of the same writer, but they are remarkably similar in style. There is nonetheless an important difference. The authentic work of the evangelist shows a flair for dramatic presentation and depth of theological penetration which are lacking in the Epistles. Thus it is correct to speak of a characteristic style of the Johannine community, which the evangelist also shares. But the evangelist is marked out from the rest by individuality and creative ability, which colour the Gospel from end to end.

John's distinctive style appears in the organisation and presentation of the material. In looking at the passages dealing with the Beloved Disciple we have seen how an item from the tradition is built up into a highly dramatic episode. Another striking example is the Raising of Lazarus in chapter 11, in which a whole series of delaying tactics holds back the climax, which at last comes as a sudden revelation to everyone present.

Similarly the discourses are steadily built up to a climax. The subject is announced, often using a saying from the tradition, as we have seen. If the dialogue form is used, the speaker may misunderstand Jesus, as in the case of Nicodemus in 3.1-10. This gives the cue for Jesus to redefine his statement, so as to take the subject to a deeper level. Another technique, which often appears in monologues, is for the evangelist or Jesus to make a sweeping statement, and then to limit its application by making a further statement which modifies it, e.g. 1.11-12; 8.15-16.

In all such cases it is the characters in the story who are ignorant of what Jesus means or of what he is leading up to. The readers are not in doubt, for they know from the first chapter who Jesus is, and so can always guess what the climax will be. This is deliberate, as it is not John's purpose to mystify the readers, but to engage their attention, so that they may be confirmed in their faith and equipped to defend it against the opponents of the church.

For this reason John is not really interested in the characters of the story except as foils to Jesus. The tendency is to use them functionally to represent different responses. We have already seen the important function of the Beloved Disciple, who typifies the evangelist's own mind and is the true follower of Jesus with whom every reader should identify. Peter's role is dictated by the tradition, which includes his confession of faith (John's version of this is in 6.69) and his three denials in the passion narrative. He thus stands for loyalty without full understanding. Thomas, as everyone knows, represents doubt about the resurrection. Andrew and Philip are missionaries. John the Baptist has the special function of witness to Jesus as the Son of God.

The character of Jesus himself in John's presentation is affected by features of the theology and style of the Gospel. Jesus is always in complete control. He knows what he will do, so that his request for information is really a test (6.6). He has insight into the characters of others (2.25; 4.16-19). In debate with his opponents he can appear petulant, especially in the discourse of 8.31-58. A more tender side to Jesus appears in the discourses on discipleship, especially when he speaks of his relationship with God in terms of loving union (14.18-24). This is most likely to be a reflection of the evangelist's own ideals.

The conclusion is inevitable that John writes at a time when the living memory of Jesus is fading, and so the portrait of Jesus is becoming more sterotyped and shaped by dogmatic considerations. The picture in the Fourth Gospel needs to be corrected by the less consciously contrived indications furnished by the Synoptic tradition. But it has its own intrinsic value, because it expresses deep thought about the meaning of Jesus by a person of outstanding ability at a creative stage in early Christianity.

Summary

In this chapter we have looked at the main problems surrounding the identity of the evangelist. It has been necessary to throw doubt on the traditional identification with the Beloved Disciple and the apostle John. But it has also been shown that there is no final consensus of scholars on this issue.

It has also appeared unsafe to presuppose that any of the Gospel is based on direct eye-witness reporting. This led to a discussion of the function of the Beloved Disciple from the point of view of the literary character of the Gospel and the evangelist's aims. It also demanded an appraisal of the available sources and their relation to the traditions in the Synoptic Gospels. It was observed that some scholars hold that John made direct use of one or more of the Synoptic Gospels. Other source theories were also reviewed.

Next the composition of the Gospel was considered. The advantage of the homiletic theory, espoused by a number of recent commentators , was shown to be in providing a credible explanation of the discourses, which are a special feature of

John. Though they are only marginally related to the sayings tradition, we saw that in nearly every case a saying of Jesus from the tradition is the 'text' of the sermon, so that it is permissible to regard them as expositions of the teaching of Jesus in relation to the special issues confronting the Johannine church.

The homiletic theory assumes that the discourses are largely based on sermons delivered over a period of time. It was also suggested that some were composed later than the the original edition of the Gospel and added to it subsequently. Many theories assume that the source materials were worked up into preliminary drafts, and some think of alternative drafts which have both found there way into the finished Gospel. If the number and variety of theories of this kind is held to count against them all, it must at least be recognised that the Gospel raises real problems of composition which cannot be solved by glossing over them.

Such questions can be disheartening to the student who is new to the serious study of John, but in fact frank recognition of them and their implications for understanding the Gospel in its setting can help to give a much greater awareness of the achievement of the evangelist. Further help can be gained by looking at the historical circumstances of the Gospel and the world of thought to which it belongs. This will be the subject of the next chapter.

Further Reading

The problem of the authorship of the Fourth Gospel is dealt with in the introductions to the standard commentaries. Martin Hengel puts this into relation with the history of the composition of all the Johannine literature in *The Johannine Question*, London: SCM Press, 1989.

Bultmann's theory of sources has been examined in detail by Dwight Moody Smith, *The Composition and Order of the Fourth Gospel. Bultmann's Literary Theory*, New Haven: Yale University Press, 1965. The same author's collected essays, *Johannine Christianity. Essays on its Setting, Sources and Theology*, Columbia (South Carolina): University of South Carolina Press, 1984, are also especially helpful.

The Signs Source has been studied by W. Nicol, *The Sēmeia in the Fourth Gospel. Tradition and Redaction*, Leiden: E.J. Brill, 1972, and especially by R.T. Fortna, *The Gospel of Signs. A Reconstruction of the*

Narrative Source Underlying the Fourth Gospel (SNTSMS 11), Cambridge: Cambridge University Press, 1970; rev. edn, 1990. Fortna's *The Fourth Gospel and its Predecessor. From Narrative Source to Present Gospel*, Edinburgh: T. & T. Clark, 1989, is a companion volume, which in my view is wrong in the attempted reconstruction of the source, but can be warmly recommended for its delineation of the theology of the present Gospel.

The claim that John is dependent on the Synoptic Gospels is made forcibly by F. Neirynck, 'John and the the Synoptics', in M. de Jonge (ed.), *L'Évangile de Jean. Sources, rédaction, théologie* (BETL 44), Leuven: Leuven University Press, 1977, pp. 73-106, and 'John and the Synoptics. 1975-1990', a paper at a symposium on *John and the Synoptics* to be published in the same series. Independence is maintained in the classic study of C.H. Dodd, *Historical Tradition in the Fourth Gospel*, Cambridge: Cambridge University Press, 1963. See also B. Lindars, *Behind the Fourth Gospel*, London: SPCK, 1971; 'Traditions behind the Fourth Gospel', in *L'Évangile de Jean*, pp. 107-124; and 'Discourse and Tradition. the Use of the Sayings of Jesus in the Discourses of the Fourth Gospel', *JSNT* 13, 1981, pp. 83-101. There is a review of the work on the Greek style of John by E. Ruckstuhl, 'Johannine Language and Style. The Question of their Unity', in *L'Évangile de Jean*, pp. 125-47. All these articles are in English, but require knowledge of Greek.

The relationship between the evangelist and the readers of the Gospel is approached from the point of view of modern literary criticism in the very readable book of R.A. Culpepper, *Anatomy of the Fourth Gospel. A Study in Literary Design*, Philadelphia. Fortress, 1983. A perceptive article which deals with various facets treated in this chapter, and is also useful for what follows, is by J.D.G. Dunn, 'Let John be John—A Gospel for its Time', in P. Stuhlmacher (ed.), *Das Evangelium und die Evangelien* (WUNT 28), Tübingen: J.C.B. Mohr, 1983, pp. 309-33.

3

THE READERS
OF THE GOSPEL

The World of John

THE IDEA THAT the Gospel of John is based on the evangelist's own homilies draws attention to the nature of the audience. But it presupposes that the Gospel was written for internal consumption in the Johannine church, whereas the closing words of 20.30-31 express an evangelistic aim. But these aims are not mutually exclusive, for the Gospel could have been written both to confirm the faith of the members of the church and to appeal to interested enquirers like Nicodemus (cf. 3.2; 7.50; 19.39). To understand the Gospel properly we need to know not only what sort of people comprised the Johannine church, but also the range of the wider audience to which it might be addressed. We shall also need to know how the Johannine Christians relate to other strands of Christianity in the first century.

There are two main avenues of research in this area. One method is to compare the Gospel with the thought of the various social and religious groups of the ancient world, noting any particular points of contact with their writings. This may help to determine what kind of people belong to the orbit of John. The other method is to search the Gospel for references to contemporary conditions. We have already seen something of this sort in the evangelist's comment on leading Jews who did not dare to commit themselves to Christian faith (12.42-43). This is an important clue to the milieu of the Gospel and the date when it was written.

Hellenistic Thought

We begin with the first of these two methods, because it has had priority in the history of the interpretation of John. As we have seen, the Gospel was first appreciated in Gnostic circles, and subsequently gained recognition in the mainstream of Christianity only very slowly. The Gnostic sects posed a threat to Christianity in the second century, because they were basically non-Christian groups which adopted Christian ideas into their teachings and claimed to possess the truth of salvation. But they are only one element in the Hellenistic world of New Testament times. Greek culture and language had spread throughout the eastern Mediterranean as a result of the conquests of Alexander the Great, including Palestine, where Greek was regularly used by the upper classes and required for diplomacy and commerce. Thus Jews, like the other peoples of the region, were necessarily affected by the wider influence of Greek philosophy and by the spread of various cults at this time. Such influence has been observed in the Jewish Wisdom literature, especially in the personification of Wisdom as a woman in Proverbs 1–9 and in Ecclesiasticus 24, which may have been developed as a counterblast to the Isis cult, and also in Wis. 7.22–8.1, which shows signs of Stoic philosophy.

1. Gnosticism is concerned with the revelation of divine knowledge to enable the soul to achieve union with the divine. As it rests on a dualist philosophy, the process of salvation requires release of the immortal soul from the prison of the body in order to ascend to the divine life. In some of the Gnostic systems the secret knowledge which solves this problem is itself the means of escape. Such knowledge might be imparted by a revealer from heaven (the saviour-myth), but this is not found in all systems. The origins of Gnosticism are probably to be traced to Hellenistic groups on the fringe of Judaism, which came into existence before they seized the Christian teaching as support for their views. A central interest was to work out the required cosmology by interpreting the Jewish creation accounts in the light of Platonist philosophy. John's Prologue was sure to attract them.

2. However, attempts to combine the creation accounts with Greek philosophy were already being made within orthodox Judaism by Philo, the Jew of Alexandria (c. 20 BCE–50 CE). His work can be compared to the aims of the Gnostics, because he interpreted all the Jewish regulations of the Law, which he faithfully observed, as helps to maintaining the intellectual raising of the mind to God. He conceived this as the union of the human mind with the wisdom or rational ordering of reality which belongs to God. To express this idea he borrowed the use of *logos* (properly = word) from Stoic philosophy, so that the *logos* of the human mind seeks harmony with the *logos* of God. The similarity of this to the Jewish Wisdom tradition extends also to the tendency to personification, so that Philo can think of God's *logos* as his offspring and image, and call it his son.

Clearly there is a certain parallel here to John's Prologue, and some scholars have thought that John was indebted to Philo. However, John shows no tendency to reproduce other aspects of Philo's enormously complex and wide-ranging thought. In particular, Philo achieved his intellectual interpretation of the Law by allegorizing the details in terms of virtues and vices, following the lead given by an earlier Alexandrian Jewish writing, *The Letter of Aristeas*. There is nothing remotely resembling this in John. The common ground between Philo and John is to be found in the Jewish Wisdom literature.

3. Another almost contemporary expression of Hellenistic religious thought is contained in the Hermetic literature, generally dated in its present form to the second century CE. In these writings Hermes Trismegistos (really a new version of the Egyptian god Thoth) is the agent of rebirth through whom humans, corrupted by lust, may be conformed to the image of the archetypal Man and so achieve the vision of God. The idea of rebirth comes into John 3.1-8, but it is entirely unnecessary to regard the evangelist's treatment of this subject as dependent on this literature.

4. If any of these currents of thought are relevant to John, it must be concluded that the Johannine church belongs to the fringe of Christianity in the New Testament period. We are already aware that a confrontation with Judaism seems to be

an ineradicable feature of the scene. A highly syncretistic milieu, in which both Jews and Christians are in contact with proto-Gnostic groups is not unthinkable. But the essentially Jewish basis of the thought of the Fourth Gospel is shown by the roots of so many of the ideas in the Old Testament. The Prologue, which shows no direct traces of Greek philosophy, is sufficiently accounted for by the Wisdom passages, and does not need the Gnostic myth of the descent of a saviour figure. The other aspect of this myth, i.e. his return (ascent) to heaven, is really part of John's *Christian* heritage, for Jesus' exaltation is an essential feature of the primitive proclamation (cf. Acts 2.36).

On the other hand our previous study of the discourses may suggest a different kind of contact with the thought represented by these groups. The evangelist is not concerned with the release of the soul from the prison of the body, but with eternal life as an experience. This takes us back to the model of Philo as an intellectual and speculative Jew. It suggests that the true relationsip between the Fourth Gospel and the Hellenistic world is to be sought in a Hellenistic-Jewish group, which is not unorthodox, but has an intellectual approach to the ancestral religion and an interest in philosophical speculation to undergird it. If that is the kind of Jewish group which is in dialogue with the Johannine church, it is likely that the church includes converts from this group in its ranks.

Qumran Thought

The idea that John was indebted to Greek thought owes its currency to the impression given by the Prologue, and was promoted in modern times by scholars who had a classical education. In spite of some dissentient voices, this view predominated in Johannine studies until the discovery of the Dead Sea Scrolls at Qumran in 1947 opened up new understanding of Judaism in New Testament times. Here were the writings of Jews, fanatically devoted to the Law, who nevertheless had a range of ideas which makes them very different from Judaism as known from the rabbinic tradition. They had vivid expectations of the coming intervention of God to conquer the forces of evil and to set up the Messianic kingdom, similar to the ideas of the apocalyptic literature of the time. But they also had a spirituality based on a moral dualism of the struggle of good and evil to gain the mastery of the human soul. Having also a highly developed angelology, they thought of warring spiritual forces, headed by the Angel of Light (also called the Spirit of Truth) and the Angel of Darkness (also called the Spirit of Falsehood). Thus the great eschatological battle is fought out at the individual level in every person.

The similarities between this and certain features of John are obvious. Though the Holy Spirit is never referred to as an angel, the same title is used (the Spirit of Truth, 14.17; 15.25; 16.13), and the chief function of the Holy Spirit is to reveal the truth. John also characterizes the devil as a dealer in falsehood (8.44). The opposition of light and darkness and the tendency to speak of good and evil in terms of truth and falsehood are both features of John which reflect Qumran. Moreover the Qumran community appears to be a sectarian body, regarding itself as possessing the monopoly of religious truth, and in this way invites comparison with the Johannine church, which is widely recognised to be sectarian in type. Its common meal for those initiated into full membership includes the blessing of bread and wine, similar to the Christian eucharist. It has also been suggested that the Johannine Christians may have observed the Qumran calendar of feasts, which differed from that of the main body of Judaism, as this might explain why John makes the Last Supper the day before the Passover in contrast with the Synoptic tradition.

Initial enthusiasm overstressed the importance of these similarities. There are also very substantial differences, notably the Qumran devotion to the Law and the pride of place given to the Zadokite priesthood. It is now recognised that the points in common with Qumran were not peculiar to the sect (probably the Essenes), but characteristic of Judaism more widely at this time. Hence the lasting effect of the discovery of the Scrolls is not to range John alongside Qumran, but to give decisive support to the Jewish character of John and the Johannine church

Qumran and the Date of John

A further consequence of the discovery of the Scrolls was that one of the obstacles to an early dating for John was removed. If the decisive influence on John was contact with Greek thought, a late date when the church was establishing itself in the Gentile world seemed to be required. But now the leading ideas of John could already be found in Jewish writings before the rise of the Christian era. This led to attempts to date John much earlier than had ever been suggested even by conservative scholars. The chief protagonist was J.A.T. Robinson, whose ideas received their fullest treatment in his magisterial book *The Priority of John* (1985).

Various factors contributed to this conclusion. It was noted that John's topography of the Holy Land was correct. John also knows Jewish customs. Moreover John has traditions not found in the Synoptic Gospels, which appear to be based on good information. We hear of a baptizing mission on the part of Jesus in 3.22 and 4.1-3, and all the events of chapters 1–3 take place in Judaea, which suggest an early phase of Jesus' ministry of which the Synoptic Gospels know nothing. We have already seen that John must have used traditions comparable to the Synoptics but independent of them. This possibility was investigated by Dodd in *Historical Tradition in the Fourth Gospel* (1964). Where there are parallels with the Synoptics (e.g. the cleansing of the temple), it is arguable that John preserves the more reliable version. So also John's timing of this incident at the very beginning of Jesus' ministry (2.13-22) instead of at the end might be correct.

The argument so far could lead to the conclusion that John had better sources than the Synoptic writers, but that would not necessarily imply an early date for the writing of the Gospel. That, however, became more possible in the light of the evidence from Qumran for the world of thought of John. Thus the evangelist's presentation of the traditions need not be regarded as any later than the date of the Synoptic Gospels, and could even be earlier. So Robinson took the final logical step and proposed that John was a redactor of primitive traditions which were superior to the Synoptic sources, making the Fourth Gospel the most reliable of all. Robinson recognized that the Gospel is the end product of a process, and did not claim that it was completed before the Synoptics, so that the 'priority' of John rests in its greater historical worth. But arguing along these lines, Robinson in the end found himself driven to the traditional position that the Beloved Disciple was to be identified with the apostle John, who was the direct source of the information reproduced by the evangelist.

Although many readers were delighted by this conservative conclusion on the part of a scholar considered to be a radical, it has not won agreement from the majority of scholars, and is unlikely to do so. Our study of the making of the Gospel in the last chapter has pointed to literary factors which are totally neglected by Robinson. Though the use of independent strands of tradition has been fully recognised, it has been necessary to recognise the vast scale of rewriting by the evangelist. It is only by denying outright John's characteristic irony that Robinson can claim that the high priest's prophecy of the destruction of temple and nation in 11.48-52 carries no allusion to the actual events of 70 CE. Further points will be considered in our next sections.

The Jews and the Pharisees

It has long been held that a date after the Jewish War is required because of John's references to the Jewish classes and parties. In spite of the good information about the Holy Land already referred to, in this matter there does seem to be an anachronism.

In the first place the most frequent designation is simply 'the Jews'. This occurs 48 times, but some cases (e.g. 'the king of the Jews' as a title for Jesus six times in the passion narrative) can be discounted. Elsewhere it is used without discrimination to mean the Jewish people, the inhabitants of Judaea, the people of Jerusalem, and the Jewish authorities in Jerusalem. In 6.41, 52, which is set in Galilee, it is not clear whether the Jews are the same as the crowd (6.22, 24) or a different audience, who might be the officials of the synagogue at Capernaum (6.59). The effect of this blanket use of the term is to differentiate Jesus from his own people in a way that is not

found in the Synoptic Gospels and is not really credible in the
historical life of Jesus.

Secondly, the Pharisees are mentioned 16 times, but the
usage in John can scarcely be regarded as correct for the
period before the Jewish War. The Pharisees were
predominantly a lay movement working for the improvement
of piety and observance of the Law among the common people.
They did, however, have members in high places, including
the Sanhedrin, so that, when John refers to 'the chief priests
and the Pharisees' (7.45; 11.47, 57; 18.3) and 'the authorities
and the Pharisees' (7.48), that is not incorrect. Josephus, the
Jewish historian, who belonged to the ruling class and
unwillingly commanded the Jewish forces in Galilee during
the Jewish War, had himself joined the Pharisees as a young
man. But because of their non-involvement the Pharisees
were not considered dangerous when the war was over, so
that they were available to fill the vacuum of leadership of the
chastened and dispirited people. Thus the Pharisees became
the leading Jews after 70 CE, and it is from their tradition that
rabbinic Judaism has developed. In the Synoptic Gospels the
Pharisees function as we should expect them to do in the
lifetime of Jesus. His conflict with them is about the application
of the Law, so that they are often mentioned alongside the
scribes. But in John the scribes are never mentioned. The
Pharisees are not clearly differentiated from 'the Jews' in the
sense of the Jewish authorities. The conclusion that the usage
in John reflects the situation when the Pharisees became the
real leaders after the disaster of the Jewish War is hard to
resist.

Thirdly, the Sadducees also are never mentioned in John.
This was the ruling Jewish party. The high priest's family and
most of the members of the Sanhedrin were Sadducees. Their
decision to yield to the pressure of the Zealots and to make war
on Rome in 66 CE proved to be their downfall, and after 70 CE
they ceased to exist. John's failure to use the name does not
necessarily imply ignorance of it, because (as in the Synoptic
Gospels) 'the chief priests' (i.e. the members of the highpriestly
families who sat in the Sanhedrin) was usually more
appropriate. But John never refers to the chief priests without

also mentioning the Pharisees, and this is surely significant in the light of what has been said above.

Church and Synagogue

John shares with the Synoptic Gospels the tradition of opposition to Jesus on the part of Pharisees and other authorities. But apart from the breaking of the sabbath (5.10; 9.14), which is clearly based on this tradition, the issues in the Fourth Gospel are completely different. As the subject of the discourses is usually an aspect of christology, it has often been held that the scenario, in which Jesus is in dispute with the Jews, is an artificial use of the traditions to provide a setting for a doctrinal debate which really belongs within Hellenistic Christianity. Largely as a result of the work of J.L. Martyn, however, it is now widely accepted that the discourses are concerned with the actual issues of the church and synagogue debate at the time when the Gospel was written. This point must be taken in conjunction with the threat of excommunication from the synagogue (9.22; 16.2), and the information in 12.42 about would-be believers who dare not commit themselves. Just as Jesus in his historic ministry was often on trial on account of the criticisms of the scribes and Pharisees, and eventually was tried by the highest authorities, so the Johannine Christians are on trial, and may have to face deprivation and even martyrdom. We do not have to postulate a late date for opposition as such. Mark's 'Little Apocalypse' already warns that 'you will be beaten in synagogues' (Mark 13.9). Thus it is not the threat of persecution which points to a later date, but the issues which are at stake.

Once we take the discourses as evidence for the Jewish and Christian debate, we can see at once that the centre of interest has shifted to aspects of christology which were not at issue in the earlier period. It appears from 9.22 that 'the Jews had already agreed that if any one should confess him to be Christ, he was to be put out of the synagogue'. This is widely held to reflect the situation towards the end of the century.

The Jews after the fall of Jerusalem were saved from despair by the efforts of the Pharisees, who made themselves into a new Sanhedrin at Javneh. They issued directives on the keeping of the Law in home and synagogue, and encouraged patience and submission to the will of God. Christians were disapproved, because they did not keep the Law and thereby 'led the people astray'. This is the complaint against Jesus in John 7.12, but it exactly corresponds with the traditional rabbinic statement preserved in *b. Sanhedrin* 43a that Jesus was 'to be stoned, because he practised magic and enticed and led Israel astray'. The full passage makes it clear that 'to be stoned' simply means to suffer the death penalty, because it goes on to say that Jesus 'was hanged (i.e. crucified) on the Preparation of the Passover'. This again tallies with the threat of stoning in John 8.59; 10.31, 39; 11.8, and also with the Johannine timing of the crucifixion. Thus John is here in touch with hostile traditions which became standard Jewish polemic after the breach between church and synagogue.

The final break is generally identified with the decision of the rabbis at Javneh to include a curse against 'the Nazareans and the Minim' in the *Amidah,* or Eighteen Benedictions, recited as a sort of creed by all worshippers in the synagogue at the opening of the sabbath service. The twelfth benediction thanks God for keeping Israel safe from her accursed enemies, with an obvious allusion to the Romans. The additional words add the Nazareans (Christians) and Minim (heretics) to these enemies. The new clause effectively excluded Christians from synagogue worship, as they could not recite the words without cursing themselves. The date of this addition is uncertain, but generally held to be about 85–90 CE. John's references to excommunication in 9.22; 12.42; 16.2 may well have some connection with this move on the part of the rabbis. In any case it is sufficient to observe that during this period relations between church and synagogue were strained to breaking-point.

The Law in John

A final indication of a fairly late date for John is to be found in the refences to the Law in the discourses. It has been suggested above that the Johannine church was in dialogue with a group of Hellenistic Jews who had an interest in the philosophical and spiritual aspects of their religion, rather like the situation of Philo. If that is the case, it is probable that John's church was recruited from this group, and this may help to explain the ambiguous relationship between them. But for our present purpose the point of interest is the spirituality of the Law to be found in this kind of group.

We usually think of the Law as a set of rules which have to be observed to maintain a person's good standing with God. It is more difficult to think of it as the focus of personal religion. But this is what it became for many Jews of the second temple period, and so it has continued to the present day. The spirituality of the Law tends to make it a mediator between God and his covenant people, because it conveys his good will and care for them and provides the means for their response. This function of the Law can be put on a philosophical footing if it is correlated with the Wisdom tradition. In the earliest relevant passage, Prov. 8.22-31, Wisdom is God's partner in creation, rejoicing in all that comes into being, and especially 'delighting in the sons of men'. So the readers are invited to receive Wisdom, for they thereby gain the key to a truly fulfilled life and receive the favour of God. In this passage the Law is not mentioned, but it does come in when this passage is rewritten by Ben Sira in Ecclesiasticus 24. For in this presentation of it the Law is identified as the highest expression of God's Wisdom.

To put this into perspective we must note that Ben Sira was a conservative, aiming to preserve the best of the national heritage of Judaism. Writing about 200–180 BCE, he was opposed to those who sought the ways of God through dreams and visions, and that means the apocalyptic movement which belongs to this period. He also distrusted the appeal to Greek philosophy, which was characteristic of the Sadducees and educated classes. Against both tendencies Ben Sira insisted that the knowledge of God and the understanding of reality were available in the Law, which embodies the whole Wisdom of God. So in Ecclus 24.1-12 Wisdom is not only God's agent in creation, but also dwells among God's people, making her earthly home in Jerusalem and the temple itself. Then in v. 23 it is stated that all her riches (recounted in vv. 13-22) 'are the book of the covenant of the Most High God, the law which Moses commanded us'. From it streams abundant Wisdom, described in the following verses in terms of the rivers of Paradise. Thus the Law is the true embodiment of the Wisdom of God.

This description has numerous points of contact with the Prologue of John, so much so that it must be regarded as the greatest single literary influence behind it. But here, instead of the Law, the fullest expression of God is in Jesus, the Word made flesh. This contrast is stated explicitly: 'The law was given through Moses; grace and truth came through Jesus Christ' (1.17). John also shares the rabbinic opposition to the attempts of visionaries to gain access to the heavenly secrets (cf. 1.18; 3.13; 5.37). Thus John's christology is worked out against a spirituality in which the Law has cosmic status as the means of salvation. It is reasonable to conclude that a Wisdom theology of this kind was a central feature of the Jewish group which was in such sharp debate with the Johannine church.

It is thus not surprising to find, as we shall see later, that in the christological discourses of John 3–10 the Law is an important factor in nearly every case. For instance in the Bread of Life discourse there is a further allusion to Ecclesiasticus 24, for in 6.35 Jesus echoes the words of Wisdom in Ecclus 24.21. Thus the opponents of John claim that the Law is the true spiritual nourishment. John counters this by asserting that Jesus is the real bread from heaven. The significance of this debate for the date of John will be clarified in the next two sections.

The Use of the Gospel in Debate

We have seen earlier that the discourses are a unique feature of the Fourth Gospel, which differentiates it from the Synoptics. We can now see that they carry the evangelist's treatment of the great issues of christology in the debate with the synagogue. But this raises the question why John used the form of a gospel to deal with it. A more detailed look at the discourses will show that John set out to anchor the argument in the Jesus tradition by building the discourses on crucial sayings of Jesus from the available sources. Thus the Christian claims about Jesus, especially the advanced christology of the Johannine church, could be shown to be consistent with the tradition. This would effectively answer the objection that the Christian claims go far beyond the commonly remembered impressions of Jesus himself. Moreover it would give assurance to the Christians themselves that their faith was soundly based in the Jesus tradition.

It is for this reason that a saying from the tradition can be detected at the start of most of the discourses. In our consideration of the discourses as homilies in the last chapter it was suggested that this is comparable to the 'text' of a sermon. Now we can see that it is the warrant for the argument which is to follow in the rest of the discourse. This point can be illustrated from the discourse with Nicodemus in John 3.

In our previous consideration of this discourse we observed that it began with a saying from the Jesus tradition which lays down the principle that a birth from above is necessary for salvation (3.3, 5). It follows from this that the revelation of divine truth must also come from above. The conclusion will be that Jesus himself, as the one who brings the divine revelation, must also have come from above in some sense (vv. 31-36). But it is now clear that, for the purpose of the debate with the unbelieving Jews, the Jewish claim that the revelation is already available in the Law must also be taken into account. This is done in 3.10-15. Here Jesus upbraids Nicodemus for being a 'teacher of Israel', who nevertheless does not have access to the truth which is necessary for salvation. No earthly person can ascend to heaven to get hold of this saving knowledge (v. 13). Very few modern readers can pick up the Old Testament allusion in this verse, but it would have been obvious to the members of the Johannine church and their Jewish rivals. It is a reference to Deut. 30.11-14, where the people's fear that God's commandment might be too hard to discover, and even need someone to go up to heaven to fetch it, is refuted on the grounds that it is available to all in the Law. For John the truth of God is fully accessible only in Jesus, and not only in Jesus as 'a teacher come from God' (v. 2), but in Jesus who was lifted up on the cross (vv. 14-15). We shall see the importance of this aspect of John's argument later. For our present purpose it is enough to recognise that the implied reference to the Law at this point confirms our observation of the pattern of the Johannine discourses: A saying from the Jesus tradition enunciates a spiritual principle. This is then shown to be inadequately catered for by the Law. Finally Jesus is shown by contrast to be the true agent of God to provide what is needed, and so to achieve salvation.

This example enables us to see that the discourses reflect real disputes with the synagogue. The conflict situation of the earlier tradition is now far more acute, and the readers can be expected to look to the Gospel to strengthen their confidence in their position. The great attention given to the theme of discipleship in chapters 13–17 shows real anxiety about the future position of the disciples in ways that reflect the ordeal which the readers themselves are passing through.

The Johannine Sect

The matters in debate between church and synagogue differed as time went on, and in John we can see traces of all the issues which were raised. In the Synoptic tradition the issue at stake is practice. There can be no doubt that this was an important point of conflict between Jesus and the scribes and Pharisees. Jesus apparently sits light to the practice of the sabbath and the rules of purity laid down in the Law and promoted by the Pharisees. John makes use of the sabbath issue in 5.9-16; 7.15-24; 9.14-16.

At the same time from the earliest days the debate was focussed on the question of Jesus' messiahship. John shows awareness of several disputed points on this issue in chapter 7. But the real centre of the debate for the Johannine church was the advanced christology which is presented in the Fourth Gospel itself, and shows Jesus as the replacement of the Law in theology and spirituality. This touches the crucial question of monotheism, which, it is claimed, is breached by John's christology (cf. 5.18; 10.33). In the eyes of the Jews the Johannine Christians were leading the people astray (7.12) and even guilty of blasphemy (10.33).

The sharpness of the debate in John suggests that the Johannine church is a beleagured sect, alienated from the local society, intensely loyal internally, but hostile to those outside. The command to love one another (13.34) gives a splendid example, but it does not extend to the opponents. Those who are within are the children of God (1.12), but the opponents are the children of the devil, who is the father of lies (8.39-47). The polarisation of categories into truth and falsehood, which we have seen to be a feature in common with the Qumran Sect, applies also to their relationship with the Jewish community, who may well have shared the same attitudes. For their opponents are evidently threatened by them and are taking drastic steps to curb their influence (15.18–16.4).

The sectarian character of the Johannine church is thus due to social pressures. Christianity started as a movement within Judaism, but gradually Christians and Jews became bitterly opposed to one another. The Johannine church is a particularly acute example of this, and it is reasonable to suggest that pressures of this kind have played a part in the development of some of the distinctive facets of John's theology.

Other Christians

The sectarian character of the Johannine church has also been attributed by modern scholars to its relationship with other Christian groups. The theory of Bultmann that John depended on a proto-Gnostic source led to the conclusion that the Johannine church adhered to a Christianized version of the saviour-myth which marked it off from mainstream Christendom. On this basis it is possible to read the Gospel as a sort of code, in which 'the Jews' are really the main body of Christians, who bitterly oppose the Johannine sect.

Starting from similar considerations, but without adopting Bultmann's theory, R.E. Brown attempted to work out the relationship with other Christian groups in his influential book, *The Community of the Beloved Disciple*. Brown takes the Beloved Disciple seriously as the founder of the Johannine tradition. In spite of the complex process which lies behind the finished Gospel, the evangelist was able to reproduce this tradition with considerable fidelity. Thus the Beloved Disciple represents Johannine Christianity in the Gospel. Other characters represent other groups. John the Baptist represents a Baptist group from which the Christians need to distance themselves. The Samaritan woman in chapter 4 represents Samaritan converts to Christianity (cf. Acts 8.5-25). This agrees with the view of Cullmann, who argues that Samaritans were a crucially important element in what he calls the Johannine circle.

The most daring feature of Brown's reconstruction is the claim that Peter in the Fourth Gospel represents mainstream, catholic Christendom over against the sectarianism of the Johannine church. Peter's position as the leader of the Twelve is acknowledged in John, but he is up-staged by the Beloved Disciple. However, this is not Brown's primary point, but rather the special character of John's christology. John shows an advance on the rest of the New Testament in giving the strongest statement of the divinity of Jesus and the clearest expression of his pre-existence. Within the Fourth Gospel itself Peter's confession of faith (6.69) stops short at saying that Jesus is 'the Holy One of God'. It is often held that the Johannine insistence on the flesh–that the Word became flesh (1.14)–is aimed at correcting a contemporary tendency to Docetism, i.e. the doctrine that Jesus only *seemed* to be human and only *seemed* to die on the cross, which is generally regarded as the earliest of the christological heresies of the second century. But if this is a necessary correction, it merely highlights the fact that in general John's own christology only too easily encourages this kind of misunderstanding, because of the distance which is placed between Jesus and the rest of mortals and the insistence that salvation, as God's gift, can come only from one who is divine.

Thus, at a time when the church was expanding in the Hellenistic world with very little central control, it is not surprising to find differences of doctrinal emphasis and the beginnings of conflict over heresies. At such a time the Johannine church might well present the appearance of an eccentric group, unwilling to be identified with the main body of Christians on account of profound disagreement on matters of doctrine. Although I find it hard to accept the idea that the character of Peter in the Fourth Gospel has anything to do with this kind of ecclesiastical situation, the possibility that the Johannine church stood apart from the main body should not be denied.

The Johannine Epistles

The dangers inherent in the christology of John become apparent in the Johannine Epistles. Brown argues that they were not written by the evangelist, but by a devoted supporter, the 'Elder', after the evangelist's death. The three letters are all addressed to an urgent situation within the Johannine church. Precisely what the evangelist had feared when composing the Prayer of Jesus in John 17 has come about. The members of the church are splitting into factions. The Elder is identified with one side in the dispute, and his purpose is to resist the dissident group. He denounces them and warns the readers against them.

The point at issue is that the dissidents 'deny that Jesus is the Christ' (1 John 2.22). They do not confess 'that Jesus Christ has come in the flesh' (1 John 4.2-3, cf. 2 John 7). Brown interprets this to mean that they separate 'Jesus' (the human Jesus) from 'the Christ' (the divinity of Jesus). In their view only his divinity matters. The result is that they think of salvation in terms of union with his divinity. They think that this union gives to them a sinless existence, and so they refuse to acknowledge their own sin or the need for atonement through the death of Jesus (1 John 1.8–2.6).

The most arresting feature of Brown's interpretation is his contention that in this acrimonious debate *both* sides claimed the support of the Gospel in support of their views. The ambiguity of the Johannine christology lends itself to opposite impressions simply by emphasis on one aspect to the exclusion of the other. The position of the dissidents shows the tendency towards Gnosticism, with its world-denying dualism and its concept of salvation as knowledge brought down from the heavenly sphere. Brown suggests that the Johannine group of churches (more than one centre is indicated by 2 and 3 John) did not survive the disruption, because it has left no trace in the known groups of the second century. The dissidents, then, are likely to have been swallowed up in one of the Gnostic sects, while the rest were absorbed in the great church.

Brown's reconstruction is not definitive, but is the best on offer. The information at our disposal is too scanty to allow certainty. One further factor still needs to be mentioned. Whereas the Gospel is preoccupied with the conflict between the church and the unbelieving Jews, there is not a trace of this in the three epistles. The reason may well be that the worsening situation attested by the Gospel (especially if 15.18–16.4 was added in a second edition) has reached the point of no return. By this time the life of the Johannine church is totally separate from its former Jewish contact. In that case, it may even have moved to a new location.

The Home of the Johannine Church

Tradition connects John with Ephesus. But this may be due to the identification of the evangelist with the John who wrote Revelation, whose connection with Ephesus is certain. Apart from this identification, which cannot be sustained, there seems to be no firm ground for locating the Gospel and Epistles at Ephesus. However, the possibility should not be excluded, because it satisfies some of the factors which need to be taken into account. (a) Though there is no direct link between the Gospel and Revelation, they have images in common, especially the Lamb of God (John 1: 29, 36; Rev. 5.6 and often) and the Water of Life (John 4.14; 7.37-38; Rev. 22.1, 17). (b) Ignatius of Antioch is our first witness to Docetism, and his letters, written at Ephesus, have echoes of Johannine diction, though he does not know the Gospel. (c) Many sects existed at Ephesus, so that it makes a suitable setting for John's contact with Hellenistic groups and other non-Christian influences. (d) There was a large Jewish community in Ephesus (cf. Acts 18.19, 24-28; 19.8-20) and a small Baptist group (Acts 19.1-7).

A possible alternative would be Syria. Ignatius was bishop of Antioch, the capital city of the province. The *Odes of Solomon,* which are poems which reflect Johannine language and ideas, are probably Syrian in origin. If the theory of influence from the proto-Gnostic group which lies behind the Mandaeans is correct, that would also indicate Syria as the point of contact.

John's reliable knowledge of Galilee and Jerusalem have persuaded some scholars that the Gospel has its origin in Palestine, but it is unlikely that the Johannine church was located there, especially if a date for the Gospel around 85–90 CE is accepted. It may be right, however, to accept connections with all three places, and assume that the community moved under pressure of circumstances from Palestine first to Syria and eventually to Ephesus. Wherever the Gospel was written, the distinctive style and diction of both Gospel and Epistles suggest a closely knit community with a tradition of its own, which would be resistant to radical change in spite of moving into new regions.

Summary

John's Gospel was written by a Christian for Christians, and the largest single influence on the evangelist was the Christian tradition. But the unique features of the Gospel demand recognition of the special circumstances which brought it into being. Aspects of the Gospel which appear to relate it to Hellenistic thought have suggested that it is a fresh presentation of the Christian message in terms of Greek thought. Thus Greek thought would have been the major influence behind the Gospel and indicate the intended readership. A similar claim for background and milieu have been made for links with proto-Gnosticism. In fact, the Hellenistic aspects of the Fourth Gospel are sufficiently accounted for in Jewish Hellenistic sources.

That the Gospel is more centrally based in Jewish thought has now become clear from the evidence of the Dead Sea Scrolls, which have furnished remarkable parallels to the Fourth Gospel. The discovery of the Scrolls also opened up the possibility of a much earlier date for the Gospel than had previously been suggested either by tradition or by critical scholarship. A crucial issue in discussion of this question is John's references to the Pharisees. Though the argument is not conclusive, on balance John's references best suit the situation of the ascendancy of the Pharisees after the Jewish War, and can be taken to reflect the readers' experience of Judaism at that time.

The Fourth Gospel was shown to reflect some of the accusations which became a standard part of the later Jewish polemic against Christians. It was also observed that references to the threat of excommunication from the synagogue best suit the conditions which led up to the situation of extreme estrangement in the last decade of the first century.

The next step was to determine the main issue between the Johannine church and the Jewish community. This was shown to be the attitude to the Law, not just in matters of practice, but especially in theology and spirituality. The basis was found in the Wisdom tradition, in which the Law is the embodiment of Wisdom. John claims that the divine Wisdom is most fully embodied in Jesus, who is the true revelation of God and agent of eternal life. In presenting this christology in the discourses, John starts from a saying of Jesus from the tradition. This gives the basic principle which lies behind the christological conclusion, and the contrast with the Law is referred to, at least by implication, in the course of the argument.

The sectarian character of the Johannine church was then attributed to the acute situation of conflict in which it was placed. It also appeared probable that the church stood apart from the mainstream of Christendom, exhibiting tendencies in christology which some would view with alarm. Though it is impossible to be sure how far the views of other Christian groups are represented in the different personalities of the Fourth Gospel, Brown's analysis of the connection between the Gospel and the subsequent disintegration of the Johannine church has much in its favour.

Brown wrote *The Community of the Beloved Disciple* with one eye on the divided state of Christendom in modern times. The history of the Johannine church shows conflict on two fronts, with the unbelieving Jews and with warring factions within. Its sectarian character is shown by the high esteem given to the love command as a feature of the in-group, which apparently does not apply to relations with those outside the group. John was alive to this danger, and strove to prevent it. John's own understanding of the gospel message rises above sectarianism to embrace all humanity. The argument that

Jesus replaces the Law as the agency of salvation is no mere polemic, but a heartfelt statement that the bounds of a nationalist faith have been broken and salvation is open to all.

Further Reading

A careful study of the various possible backgrounds of thought is given by C.H. Dodd, *The Interpretation of the Fourth Gospel*, Cambridge: CUP, 1953, which is still useful, though it does not take into account the Dead Sea Scrolls, which were then only recently published.

The question of Gnostic influence is considered in relation to the New Testament as a whole by E. Yamauchi, *Pre-Christian Gnosticism: A Survey of the Proposed Evidence*, London: Tyndale, 1973, and by R. McL. Wilson, *Gnosis and the New Testament*, Oxford: Blackwell, 1968. The modern discovery of Gnostic texts at Nag Hammadi has reopened the discussion of the influence on John, and one tract, generally known as 'The Trimorphic Protennoia', must be either dependent on John or the other way round. It is usefully discussed by Y. Janssens, 'The Trimorphic Protennoia and the Fourth Gospel', in *The New Testament and Gnosis: Essays in Honour of R. McL. Wilson* (ed. A.H.B. Logan and A.J.M. Wedderburn), Edinburgh: T. & T. Clark, 1983, pp. 229-44.

The relationship between John and the Dead Sea Scrolls is the subject of the collection of essays by various writers, *John and Qumran* (ed. J.H. Charlesworth), London: Chapman, 1972. The fullest translation of the Scrolls is that of G. Vermes, *The Dead Sea Scrolls in English*, London: Penguin, [3]1987. This third edition has the 'Songs for the Holocaust for the Sabbath' (pp. 220-30), which shows the influence of the Jewish mystical tradition, which claims to penetrate the heavenly secrets.

The case for an early date for the Gospel of John is argued most fully by J.A.T. Robinson, *The Priority of John*, London: SCM Press, 1985. A date much closer to the final split between church and synagogue is convincingly argued by J.L. Martyn, *History and Theology in the Fourth Gospel*, Nashville: Abingdon, [2]1979. Other related issues are considered in the essays of C.K. Barrett, *The Gospel of John and Judaism*, London: SPCK, 1975.

The history and character of the Johannine church are reconstructed in the important study of R.E. Brown, *TheCommunity of the Beloved Disciple*, London: Chapman, 1979. Other relevant books are O. Cullmann, *The Johannine Circle*, London: SCM Press, 1976, and R.A. Culpepper, *The Johannine School*, Missoula: Scholars Press, 1975. A brief and very readable analysis of the way in which the whole Gospel reflects the tense situation between church and synagogue is provided by A.E. Harvey, *Jesus on Trial*, London: SPCK, 1976.

4

UNDERSTANDING
JOHN

Asking the Right Questions

THE GOSPEL OF JOHN is not just a biography, but a theological interpretation of Jesus to promote faith. It has survived the situation of conflict in which it was written, and the subsequent demise of the Johannine community, to become one of the most highly valued books of the Bible. It may be claimed that the Fourth Gospel can be read with profit without the paraphernalia of scholarship, and of course this is true up to a point. But our study of the complex questions relating to the author and the readers in the last two chapters have shown that factual matters and understanding are inextricably intertwined. We have already had to trespass on the territory which now lies before us, as we approach the theology of the Fourth Gospel and its meaning for today.

The task of understanding will be eased if the right questions are put to the text. In the first chapter it was pointed out that people often approach John with the wrong expectations. It is obvious that the author's purpose needs to be appreciated first in tackling any book. We have not only looked into this in the case of John, but also seen how this purpose is achieved through the skilful construction of both narrative and discourse in relation to the needs of the Johannine church.

Seeing that the purpose of John is to promote belief in order that the readers may have 'life', we can see at once that one reason why the Fourth Gospel differs radically from the Synoptic Gospels is that it is addressed to people whose concept of what constitutes salvation differs from that of the mainstream of earliest Christianity. This, then, is the best point from which to begin our investigation. Salvation is the end to which the whole presentation of the Gospel is directed, and it controls the structure of the evangelist's theology. And, of course, it is the real issue in the debate with the opponents of the Johannine church.

The Concept of Salvation

The chief clue to the distinctive character of John's concept of salvation is the use of 'life' or 'eternal life' instead of 'the kingdom of God' or 'the kingdom of heaven'. Only in 3.3, 5 is 'the kingdom of God' used, and that, as we have seen, is a version of a traditional saying of Jesus (cf. Matt. 18.3; Mark 10.15). When the idea is taken up in the discourse which it introduces, it becomes 'eternal life' (3.15, 16, 36). It is the reason for God's action in Christ, unforgettably expressed in the 'miniature gospel' of 3.16: 'For God so loved the world that he gave his only Son, that whoever believes in him should not perish but have eternal life'.

It seems, then, that the evangelist and the readers are not vitally interested in the notion of the kingdom of God, even though it was frequently on the lips of Jesus himself. To understand this change we must look first at the phrase in the teaching of Jesus and earliest Christianity. It properly denotes the rule of God, and in certain contexts it can even be a substitute-word for God himself (thus 'the kingdom of heaven is at hand' can mean 'God is near', referring to his eschatological coming). The preaching of Jesus is specially concerned with preparing his audience for the coming of the kingdom in this sense, as a future event which is expected imminently. His moral teaching is set in the context of a testing confrontation with God. In readiness for this he turns attention to the springs of action in the heart. At the same time he proclaims that the coming action of God will prove to be the arrival of blessing for the poor and despised. Thus salvation consists in surviving the coming ordeal and enjoying the eschatological kingdom of God which lies beyond it.

This teaching of Jesus is in line with widespread hopes and expectations in his time. Both the Dead Sea Scrolls and the contemporary apocalyptic literature presuppose that the present time is the last generation before the final act of God to set up the everlasting kingdom. It is possible to distinguish between a popular political concept, which expresses the hope of liberation from the Roman power and the setting up of the messianic kingdom on earth, and a more esoteric transcendental concept, which looks for a cataclysmic intervention by God and the start of a new age, indeed a new creation, in which God will reign supreme. As a prophet and visionary, Jesus most likely held a view comparable to the second scheme rather than the first (which would make him politically dangerous). But his audience evidently cherished hopes of the first kind, and this explains why he was reticent about making a messianic claim, though in the end this was the charge on which he was convicted and crucified.

This concept of salvation is thus a practical matter. It is a coming state of blessedness, in which all will observe the high morality which befits God's kingdom. It does not necessarily entail abrogation of the Jewish Law, but rather a state in which that will be perfectly fulfilled. The famous prophecy of the new covenant in Jer. 31.31-34 (perhaps referred to by Jesus himself at the Last Supper, Mark 14.24; 1 Cor. 11.25), exactly expresses this. Jesus expects this new state of affairs to be ushered in by God himself on the coming great day, and not to be brought about by human intervention.

Realised Eschatology

This concept of salvation was naturally reaffirmed by the primitive Christian community. The only new factor was that Jesus was proclaimed to be risen and exalted as the Messiah in heaven, where he is ready to act as God's agent in the inauguration of the everlasting kingdom.

The idea of a future divine act is generally referred to as 'consistent eschatology', in the sense that statements concerning the future are logically consistent and really refer to the future. But some aspects of Jesus' teaching suggest that the future conditions are already available (cf. Matt. 12.28;

Luke 17.21). How far such sayings mean that the future is
already realised in the present (realised eschatology) is
disputed. He may have meant only that anticipations of the
conditions which belong to the future are already apparent,
and these reinforce the claim that the coming kingdom is
near.

The apostolic proclamation, however, inevitably introduced
a new dimension. Jesus, exalted and enthroned at the right
hand of God, already has his rightful position in the future
kingdom. So now the idea of salvation has two poles. The
kingdom in the full sense still belongs to the future, but it is
present in so far as Jesus is acknowledged as Lord. So the
conditions of the future already operate in the life of the
church under his heavenly lordship.

This interim period before God's final act was not expected
to last long. Paul (Rom. 13.11-12; 1 Cor. 7.29) and the author
of Hebrews (10.25, 37) still expect the end imminently. But as
time passed by and still Jesus' coming (the parousia) did not
take place, it became necessary to settle for indefinite delay. In
fact, the key to coping with the problem was already available
in the concept of the present lordship of Jesus. If people die
before the parousia, that does not mean that they lose their
share in the coming kingdom, for their souls go to a place of
waiting (Rev. 6.9-11) close to Jesus (Phil. 1.23), whether the
time be long or short (1 Thess. 4.13-17).

This view of the programme of salvation is not strictly
realised eschatology, because it does not imply that the future
is wholly swallowed up in the present. It is much more an
anticipated eschatology, and its crucial feature is the dynamic
concept of salvation now, but not yet. Christians live in the
conditions of the coming age, but at the same time look
forward to the consummation when Jesus will come in glory
as God's agent for the general resurrection and the judgment.

Life and Eternal Life in John

How, then, are we to understand John's concept of salvation
against this background? It is often claimed that the evangelist
teaches a realised eschatology in the strict sense, rejecting the
idea of a future divine act. Bultmann's existential inter-

pretation of the Gospel sees life as 'authentic existence', which results from the act of faith in Jesus (cf. 3.15-16). But this excludes Johannine expressions of consistent eschatology (e.g. 5.25-29), which Bultmann had to attribute to a subsequent Ecclesiastical Redactor. But the matter is not so simple as this, for consistent eschatology is basic to the argument of passages which Bultmann does accept. Thus the discourse of 5.19-47 uses a parable from the tradition (v. 19) to argue that God's Son is his agent for the eschatological acts of the general resurrection (v. 21) and the judgment (v. 22), and therefore should receive the same honour as the Father (v. 23). As the Son is identified with Jesus, faith in him makes available now the state of salvation which is due to follow these acts (v. 24). He does not say that these acts will not happen at all.

It is reasonable to conclude from this and other passages that the Fourth Gospel has the same dynamic concept of 'now, but not yet' as we can already see in Paul. Eternal life means life that belongs to the coming age (= *ha-'olam ha-ba* in rabbinic sources). The Hebrew *'olam* means 'lasting state', and so can refer either to eternity or to an epoch of time. The phrase can thus be used as a substitute for the kingdom of God, placing the emphasis not on his rule, but on his eternity. The Greek translation *aiōn* tends to emphasise the notion of eternity still further. There is an instructive example in Mark 10.30, where Jesus promises rich rewards in this life 'and in the age (*aiōn*) that is coming eternal (*aiōnios*) life'.

John's preference for this expression shows a decisive shift away from the future reference, but without denying it altogether, as we have seen. But John is more concerned with the present experience of life in the rich sense suggested by 10.10. This life is eternal in as much as it belongs also to the coming age, and so lasts on without ending. Salvation is thus the possession of such life both now and eternally.

Thus John's concept of salvation does not dissolve the future entirely in a timeless present, and to that extent it is in line with the mainstream Christian tradition. We must assume that what appears to be a more timeless way of speaking is used because it is more meaningful to evangelist and readers alike, and also to the Jews with whom they are in dialogue. They are people who do not need liberation from poverty and

political oppression, but from false ideas about the attainment
of eternal life.

A New Dimension

With this concept of salvation in mind, we can see that the
theology of John is chiefly concerned with showing how Jesus
is the effective agent of salvation for all who will believe in him.
In the Fourth Gospel, as we have seen, this function of Jesus is
contrasted with the Law, which the opponents claim is the
true means of life. But in John's view believing in Jesus
introduces a new dimension, which cannot be found in the
Law. This is perhaps best expressed in modern terms as the
category of personal relationship.

This is really the distinguishing feature of the teaching of
Jesus, and explains his conflict with the scribes and Pharisees.
Without in any way denying the Law, Jesus made the state of
the heart the decisive factor rather than the letter of the Law.
In prayer he encouraged a simple directness, exemplified in
his own address to God as 'Father', without honorific titles.
The idea of the coming of God, usually depicted in horrific
terms in contemporary apocalyptic, becomes something to be
welcomed. No one need fear the judgment of God except those
who obdurately refuse to open their hearts to receive him.

After the resurrection this aspect of Jesus' teaching was
maintained by a strong sense of fellowship with him in his
glory. Baptism into the name of Jesus meant initiation into the
company of those who confess him as Messiah and Lord.
From a very early date, perhaps from the beginning,
Christians began to invoke him as their heavenly leader, using
the formula *marana tha:* 'Our Lord, come!' (1 Cor. 16.22, cf.
Rev. 22.20). The sense of fellowship with Jesus made it possible
to follow his own simple approach to God, addressing him as
'Abba, Father' (Rom. 8.15; Gal. 4.6).

This sense of personal fellowship with Jesus, and through
him with God, is also a feature of John. It is especially
represented in 14.18-24, where Jesus speaks of his future
relationship with the disciples. Here there are two overlapping
unities, of the Father with Jesus and of Jesus with the disciples
(v. 20).

The chief phrase used to express this relationship in John is to 'believe in (literally, into) Jesus'. This means to entrust oneself to Jesus, fully accepting what he proclaims himself to be. The phrase is unusual, but it does occur eight times elsewhere in the New Testament besides the 36 cases in the Gospel of John and 3 cases in 1 John. It is not found in the Septuagint or in secular Greek. Evidently it is not confined to the evangelist, but should rather be seen as characteristic diction of the Johannine church.

The phrase is important for the theology of the Fourth Gospel, because it can be used only with a personal object. It would be unthinkable to 'believe into' the Law. It makes of Jesus a personal mediator between the believer and God, whereas the Law, however much it is a testimony to the grace of God (1.16), is essentially an impersonal instrument.

On the other hand, those whose spirituality is centred on the Law as the embodiment of the Wisdom of God, obviously find in it great riches (cf. Ecclus 24.25-34), and will not easily be convinced that the gospel of Jesus has more to offer. Moreover, if the teaching of Jesus led to conflict with the Pharisees, Christian teaching about Jesus also leads to conflict, because it seems to lead the people astray by down-grading the Law, and the position accorded to Jesus almost makes of him a second god, which would be blasphemy (5.18; 7.12; 10.33). The theology, however, which John sets forth in the Prologue and the discourses of the Gospel has an answer to both these points. The dimension of personality turns out to be crucial.

The Prologue

The Prologue (1.1-18) has been the subject of an immense number of studies. It has been claimed to be a pre-Johannine Semitic poem, and many attempts have been made to reconstruct what might have been its original form. From a literary point of view there is much to be said for two basic observations: it is a distinct composition in the style of Semitic Wisdom poems, even if not actually written as poetry, and the intruded verses in prose on John the Baptist (vv. 6-8, 15) have been meshed into it in the course of its incorporation into the Gospel. However, there is no compelling reason to regard it as older than the Gospel, or as composed by a different hand. In my view, it was added as part of the second edition to give the rationale of the christology which is everywhere assumed in the Gospel, though not elsewhere stated in philosophical terms. As a composition in the style of the Wisdom poems, it need not be regarded as based on any more specific model. It has already been pointed out that it has its closest parallel in Ecclesiasticus 24.

The crucial point in the Prologue is v. 14: 'And the Word became flesh'. This is the first clear statement of the incarnation, which became a fundamental doctrine of Christianity, but has been the subject of immense controversy. Obviously this cannot be followed up here, and we must be content with trying to answer two questions: Where did the evangelist get the idea from, and what does it actually mean?

The first question cannot be answered by those who look for the origin of John's ideas in Greek or Gnostic sources. Greek religion knows of gods who appear as human beings (cf. Acts 14.11-12) and of supermen who are raised to the company of the gods (as in the emperor cult), but not of a divine being who becomes actually human and mortal. Gnostic dualism, totally separating the divine from the human, cannot entertain the notion of incarnation. It is the Wisdom tradition of Hellenistic Judaism which offers the best solution, as nearly all modern scholars agree. This can be traced in the New Testament through Paul (1 Cor. 1.30), the 'Colossian hymn', Col. 1.15-20 (possibly post-Pauline), and the opening verses of Hebrews (1.1-4), in which Wisdom as God's Son is his agent in creation and active in Jesus in the work of redemption.

John's statement that the Word became flesh is only marginally different from this. Instead of saying that the Word/Wisdom/Son of God was active in Jesus, John says that it was embodied (became flesh) in Jesus. I believe that this slight difference arises from the use of the Ecclesiasticus poem. There the Wisdom of God is embodied in the Law; it *is* the Law (Ecclus 24.23). John agrees up to a point; but the fulness of God's self-revelation is available only in Jesus (v. 18). It thus seems likely that the inspiration for the ground-breaking claim in v. 14 is the Ecclesiasticus poem, which has been the catalyst of a new dimension of christology as a result of John's preoccupation with claims concerning the Law.

With regard to the second question, we have to bear in mind the Semitic tendency to personify abstracts. Wisdom is *God's* wisdom, an attribute of God. It is by *his* skill that the world was made. When this property of God is personified, it is usually personified as a woman, because the word for wisdom is feminine in both Hebrew and Greek. But the same idea can be expressed by referring to the Word of God as his agent in creation (cf. Ps. 33.6). This gives a masculine alternative (Greek *logos*), which also lends itself to personification, so that in Philo God's Word is even referred to as his 'firstborn son' (*Agr. Noe* 12), without any suggestion of a 'second god'. But when, as in the Fourth Gospel (and already in Colossians and Hebrews), God's Wisdom/Word/Son is said to be active in the person of Jesus, or even incarnate in him, the way is open for a subtle shift from the *metaphorical* language of personification to the *metaphysical* concept of personal relations within God himself, such as John has attempted to set out in vv. 1-2 of the Prologue. John's position becomes clearer when we see how it relates to the contrast with the Law. If the Law is the embodiment of God's Wisdom, it can be said to have been with him as an idea in his mind from the beginning, before it 'became incarnate' in its written form as given to Moses on Mount Sinai. In fact rabbinic tradition asserts that the Law is one of seven pre-existent things in this way. So also Jesus, as the embodiment of God's eternal Word, is the pre-existent Son of God.

It is important to realise that John's concept of the pre-existence of Jesus carries no implication that he is anything less than fully and truly human. Though the living memory of Jesus was disappearing by the time that the Gospel was written, the anchorage in the record of Jesus as a man of recent history is unquestioned, and his death is real, and would be inexplicable without his real humanity. It may seem extraordinary for John to make Jesus speak of his relationship with God before the foundation of the world (17.5, 24) and claim that 'Before Abraham was, I am' (8.58), but the whole point of the Prologue is to explain how this could be so.

Nevertheless the concept of incarnation is so daring that it is not at all surprising that the Jewish opponents sensed here a threat to monotheism. However, it must be made clear that John's doctrine of incarnation did not *start* the accusation that the Christians were treating Jesus as God (5.18; 10.33). In fact, quite the opposite is the case, because the Prologue is an attempt to provide a rational explanation of existing Christian practice so as to show that the complaint is unfounded. What started it was the claim that, having been exalted to God's right hand as the Messiah, Jesus was worthy of equal honour (5.23), and the offending practice was the custom of invoking Jesus in that position, which we can see in the *marana tha* prayer (1 Cor. 16.22). This is the step, taken in the earliest days of Christianity but unprecedented in Judaism, which set Christianity on its unique course.

Incarnation

The basic historic fact is that Jesus was a man who died by crucifixion under the governorship of Pontius Pilate. We shall see later that it is this fact which in John's view proves that Jesus is the Son of God. But there is no suggestion in the Fourth Gospel that, because he is the Son of God, he did not really die. In so far as Jesus is represented as aware that he will rise from the dead, this is because Jesus knows God's plan of redemption and so has faith that his death will be abundantly fruitful (11.54; 12.24). When Jesus performs miracles, these are human acts done by divine inspiration, like the miracles of Elijah or Elisha. But at the same time they are 'works of God' (5.36), because they signify God's saving plan to bring healing and eternal life to all humanity. Similarly, Jesus' remarkable insight into people's minds is a human characteristic, and the woman of Samaria is correct in drawing the conclusion that Jesus must be a prophet (4.19). Such power of insight would be considered normal in a prophet.

Hence it is entirely wrong to separate acts of Jesus which proceed from his divine nature and acts which proceed from his human nature, as was done by some of the church fathers in interpreting the Fourth Gospel. All his acts are fully human, but in and through them there is the Word of God, declaring their meaning for salvation. In this sense they are all divine acts at the same time. The pre-existent Son/Wisdom/Word of God, who perpetually communes with God, being in the bosom of the Father (1.18), does his communing in and through Jesus, and so Jesus always does what is pleasing to the Father (8.29).

The Old Testament in John

Before we leave the Prologue we must note the allusions to other parts of the Old Testament. The opening verses have an obvious relation to Gen. 1.1-4, which is clearly intentional. Much more important are the allusions to the giving of the Law to Moses in vv. 14-18. In saying 'we have beheld his glory' (v. 14), the evangelist knows that the readers are sure to think of Moses' request to God in Exod. 33.18: 'Show me your glory.' The glory which the eye of faith perceives in Jesus as the incarnate Word is 'full of grace and truth.' These words are based on God's self-revelation to Moses as the Lord 'abounding in steadfast love and faithfulness' (Exod. 34.6). Later Jewish tradition insisted that this was not direct sight of God (v. 18, cf. 5.37). For John, only Jesus makes God fully known, and this the Law could never do.

However, John has a positive attitude to the Law from the point of view of its prophetic value. This carries forward the conviction of earliest Christianity that all the scriptures of the Old Testament are prophetic of the plan of salvation. Matthew frequently inserts proof-texts with the formula 'that what was spoken by the prophet might be fulfilled' (e.g. Matt. 4.13). Significantly John uses an almost identical formula (e.g. 12.38) and has some of the very same texts. Thus there is a debt in the Fourth Gospel to the use of Scripture in debate with Jews, which was common to all branches of the primitive church from the earliest times.

The chief sources of texts quoted in this way are the Prophets and Psalms. This is characteristic not only of earliest Christianity, but also of the Scrolls, which use similar techniques of quotation, including some of the same texts, in relation to the Qumran Sect itself. The theory is that in the

Scriptures God has made known in advance the programme of the end time, which is now on the brink of fulfilment.

This concept of fulfilment is not confined to specific quotations from Scripture, but pervades most of the scriptural allusions throughout the Gospel. This applies to the references to Moses in the Prologue which we have just seen. The revelation of God in Jesus as the incarnate Word is not only better than the revelation to Moses in the Law. It is also the fulfilment of that earlier revelation in the order of redemption.

Jesus' Qualifications

The main discourses which follow in chapters 3–10 are concerned with Jesus' qualifications for his function as the agent of God's final act of redemption, and give an idea of the way in which he performs it.

The Nicodemus discourse of chapter 3 makes the basic point that the act of salvation depends on the initiative of God, and therefore the agent of salvation himself must originate from God. As God's agent to fulfil his own plan of salvation he was God's Son given to the world (3.16). The giving of God's Son surpasses the gift of the Law, because that did not make accessible the image and glory of God, as has been done in Jesus (3.13). Only of him can it be said that 'The Father loves the Son, and has given all things into his hand' (3.35). What, then, does Jesus convey which is not available in the Law? The answer is not simply that, as a person, he conveys the knowledge of God in personal terms, but that in his humanity he was lifted up on the cross (3.14). This point will prove to have decisive importance in later chapters.

The discourse with the Samaritan woman in chapter 4 presupposes that Jesus is the agent of salvation, but expresses it in different terms. The water of life is of course a metaphor used in the Wisdom tradition, and is applied in Ecclesiasticus 24 to the inexhaustible supply of Wisdom which is available in the Law. Though the Samaritans were really Jews and kept the Law according to their own customs, John uses them to represent the wider world. In particular John takes up the Samaritan concept of the Messiah, which is more the expectation of the true teacher. Jesus, as the mediator of the living water of the divine Wisdom, is qualified to be the fulfilment of Samaritan hopes, and by implication those of the whole world (4.42). Though the point is not brought to the surface, the discourse suggests that another reason why Jesus surpasses the Law is the universality of the gospel.

In the discourse of chapter 5 the point at issue is the authority of Jesus to override the law of the sabbath. The argument turns on the fact that Jesus' act of healing on the sabbath is a model of the eschatological acts which he is destined to perform. Indeed, through such acts the future condition of eternal life is already accessible to believers (5.21-24). Jesus' authority is grounded in the fact that his acts are always done in accordance with the instructions of his Father (5.19). Thus he does not rely on human authorisation, or even on the witness of John the Baptist (5.36). There is witness to his authority, however, in the Scriptures, because they are prophetic of the eschatological age, and in the Law itself Moses 'wrote of' Jesus in this sense (5.46).

The Bread of Life discourse of chapter 6 clearly builds on the Wisdom theme of the nourishment of the soul. The argument is based on the manna miracle of Exodus 16. In John's milieu the Wisdom which the manna typifies is contained in the Law. This explains the reference to teaching in v. 45, quoting a passage of Isaiah in which the metaphor of abundant spiritual food is also present (Isa. 54.11–55.5). Of course Jesus surpasses the Law in this respect. The proof of this is his saving death, subtly referred to in vv. 53-58 by means of the eucharistic tradition of Jesus' Body and Blood. For the eucharist is the ceremony in which the saving death of Jesus is proclaimed (1 Cor. 11.26). Though denied by some scholars, the whole discourse has eucharistic overtones from start to finish. The Christian eucharist provides spiritual as well as physical nourishment because it is the celebration of Jesus' *death,* and *that* is what makes him the true bread in a way that the Law can never be.

The episodic discourse of 7.1–8.30 combines the theme of the necessity of Jesus' death with the question whether he has the proper credentials for messiahship. It is implied that he does have them, but his death is more important. The death is referred to cryptically in the idea of 'going away' (7.32-36;

8.14, 21-22), but becomes explicit in the reference to lifting up in the saying of 8.28. The Law is adduced in 7.15-24 and in 8.12-20, which takes up the theme of witness from chapter 5. Jesus, still refusing to accept human witness, declares that the legal requirement for two witnesses to support a case is met by the agreement between himself and the Father. This at last opens the way to understanding the importance of the crucifixion, because the cross demonstrates the unity between Jesus and the Father (8.29).

The short and sharp discourse of 8.31-59 presents Jesus' opponents as children of the devil by contrast with Jesus' own affiliation to God. The point of this contrast appears in a saying from the Jesus tradition in 8.51, 52 (cf. Mark 9.1). As God's Son, Jesus can give eternal life, because he has life in himself, for indeed he is pre-existent (v. 58). Though the Law is not mentioned, it is clear that the Jews, who have the Law and rely on their descent from Abraham as the covenant people (8.39), do not have the capacity to give life which is claimed by Jesus, and which will be demonstrated in his death and resurrection.

The story of the Man Born Blind in chapter 9 is really preparatory to the climax in the next chapter, contrasting the sight which Jesus gives (in fact, creates) with the spiritual blindness of the Pharisees. In *the Allegory of the Shepherd in 10.1-18* Jesus is contrasted with all predecessors (v. 8), and then proclaims himself the Good Shepherd who gives his life for the sheep. This is the point which was made at the end of the discourse in 8.28-29, and it enables John to heighten the emotional force of the climax in 10.22-30, where Jesus' saving action for the sake of the 'sheep' is the final proof that he and the Father are one (v. 30). Thus Jesus' unique relationship with God is stated in the simplest possible terms. To the protest of 'blasphemy' he makes recourse once more to the Scriptures ('your law', v. 34), making what many readers feel to be a dubious debating-point. But the real point is that, by perceiving the true meaning of Jesus' 'works', i.e. his whole earthly ministry, the opponents 'may know and understand that the Father is in me and I am in the Father' (10.38). That is his real qualification, and that is how he is able to effect salvation.

The Death of Jesus

The death of Jesus thus turns out to be the decisive factor of the whole argument, just as it is the climax of the narrative structure of the Gospel as a whole. This point needs to be made strongly, because the Fourth Gospel is so often thought of as the gospel of the incarnation that the death of Jesus tends to be neglected. But in our consideration of the incarnation above, it was pointed out that for John it is the death of Jesus which is the real proof that he is the pre-existent Son of God.

The starting point is the voluntary character of Jesus' death. John rightly saw that, though Jesus was condemned to death, it was in one sense entirely voluntary, because he could have saved himself by retracting his message. Jesus lays down his life of his own accord, and the power to take it up again (i.e. the resurrection) simply follows on from the power to lay it down (10.18). The two acts are really two sides of a single coin, as we shall see in a moment. Jesus says, 'For this reason the Father loves me' (10.17), because his acceptance of death is his freely willed choice to obey the charge given by the Father. In giving his life for the sheep he demonstrates not just his own pastoral care, but the Father's own will for the salvation of all people (10.29). This makes it plain for all to see that he is at one with the Father (10.30).

John places great emphasis on the demonstrative aspect of the cross (cf. 8.28). The reason is given in 3.14, where the idea of lifting up the Son of Man is first introduced. Many scholars detect a double meaning in the idea of 'lifting up'. Literally it refers to the cross, but theologically it refers to the exaltation of Jesus to heaven. If this is correct, it probably entails a reference to Isa. 52.13, the introduction to the prophecy of the Suffering Servant, which tells of his exaltation after his humiliation even to death (the same Greek word is used for 'lifted up'). It is then exaltation in the eyes of the world. The world can *see* the exaltation of Jesus in the crucifixion, not because of a juggling with the meaning of a word, but because what is actually seen in that horrifying event is the ultimate demonstration of his moral union with the Father, which *also* issues in his exaltation to God's right hand (hence 'glorified' is used instead of 'lifted up' in 12.23; 13.31).

The death of Jesus is at the same time the supreme moral victory in the flesh. Jesus' personal wishes and his natural shrinking from death are totally subordinated to the will of God (12.27-30). Thus in his person the devil's grip on humanity is broken. The victory over 'the prince of this world' is won (12.31). Thus this historic event is at the same time the cosmic victory which is needed to usher in the eschatological age.

John also carries forward the traditional interpretation of Jesus' death as an atonement sacrifice which belongs to earliest Christianity (cf. 1 Cor. 15.3), and which is accepted in the Johannine church (1 John 2.2). So it is referred to in the testimony of John the Baptist (1.29, 35). Jesus gives his life *for* the life of the world (6.51), *for* the sheep (10.11, 15), *for* his friends (15.13).

Atonement is not stressed in the Fourth Gospel, however, because the essential point for the argument is the concept of Jesus' union with the Father. This is demonstrated in the cross, and once this is grasped by the believer, the way is opened to enter into personal relationship with God through Jesus. The death of Jesus is what 'draws' people to believe in him (12.32), and believing in him is precisely the personal relationship in which salvation is experienced. Thus the cross is the high point of the revelation of God's love, and his love is what effects salvation.

The Son of Man

Each time John uses the 'lifting up' theme Jesus refers to himself as the Son of Man. This title is used by Jesus frequently in the Synoptic Gospels. The exact meaning of the phrase in the sayings of Jesus has been the subject of endless controversy. This can be touched on here only briefly, and we shall have to be content with trying to understand the use in John, and especially why it is so prominent in connection with the cross.

Son of Man occurs in the Gospels only in sayings attributed to Jesus, or in reference to them. It is never used as a title for Jesus in christology outside the Gospels, except in Acts 7.56 (which may be modelled on a gospel saying). 'Son of man' in

Aramaic just means a man or a human being, or it may be used collectively for people. The three occurrences outside the Gospels and Acts have this meaning, all in biblical quotations (Heb. 2.6 = Ps. 8.4; Rev. 1.13 and 14.14 = Dan. 7.13). So when Jesus used it as an impersonal reference to himself, it would seem obvious that it should mean 'a man like me' (cf. Matt. 8.20 = Luke 9.58).

Unfortunately the matter is complicated because of the interpretation of Dan. 7.13. In Daniel's vision power is given to 'one like a son of man', i.e. a human figure, after all the beasts (= enemies of the Jews) have been brought into subjection. In Jewish interpretation in New Testament times this man-like figure is identified with the Messiah. For this reason it is widely held to be a messianic title. Synoptic sayings attributed to Jesus which speak of his future glory often combine the designation Son of Man with clear allusions to Dan. 7.13 (e.g. Matt. 24.30). But the question whether Jesus himself intended to make a messianic claim when he used this phrase as a title, or whether all the relevant sayings which suggest this are inauthentic, remains hotly disputed.

For our present purpose it is sufficient to notice two things. First, even if many sayings are inauthentic, enough are so well embedded in the tradition that Jesus' use of Son of Man to refer to himself in some sense can be safely regarded as a genuine characteristic of his style. John has picked it up from the sayings tradition. Secondly, in the Synoptic tradition the phrase is used in Jesus' predictions of the passion (e.g. Mark 8.31). Here again it is disputed whether this means 'the Messiah must suffer' or 'I must suffer' or (ironically) 'a man must suffer', meaning oneself.

The use in the Fourth Gospel is certainly a matter of adopting the phrase as a style-feature, and closer examination of all the occurrences suggests that they are modelled primarily on the passion predictions. It has been argued by Smalley that they are all based on traditional sayings, but this is difficult to prove. The connection with the passion predictions can be seen in 3.14, where John's word 'must' is reminiscent of Mark 8.31, and this connection can be followed through in 8.28; 12.23, 34; 13.31, all referring to the lifting up or glorification of the Son of Man. In the light of our study of the death of Jesus in the Fourth Gospel, it is altogether probable that the phrase is used in these examples not as a messianic title but precisely because the death is a *human* act. It is the supreme moment in the human life of Jesus when his union with the Father is demonstrated.

This provides the key to understanding the other Son of Man sayings in John. The phrase is not a title, but functional. Thus the programmatic statement of 1.51 tells of a future occasion when heaven will be joined to earth, 'the angels of God ascending and descending upon the Son of man'. It is a human event in which heavenly glory will be revealed. This must surely be the crucifixion. 3.13 tells of the revelatory function of the Son of Man, and this is immediately elucidated in the reference to the cross in 3.14. If this functional use of the Son of Man is borne in mind, it becomes apparent that the Fourth Gospel has a specialised use of the phrase, which is closely integrated into the Johannine theology. It refers to the human death of Jesus, which is the earthly point of revelation of his divine glory.

The 'I am' Sayings

In the climactic saying of 8.28 Jesus not only mentions the lifting up of the Son of Man, but also asserts that as a result of it 'you will know that I am he.' The phrase 'I am he' is literally 'I am' (*egō eimi*). It is one of a number of 'I am' sayings, which are nearly always quite striking in their context and constantly attract the attention of readers of the Gospel. It is often claimed that they have special importance in the structure of John's theology, but two reasons suggest that they should not be given undue weight.

In the first place they are very unevenly distributed, and do not usually form the climax of an argument. Obviously an 'I am' saying is a statement of who Jesus is, and the identity of Jesus is the great topic of *all* the discourses. But in most of the discourses to try to give these sayings climactic significance only leads to distortion of the argument and obscures their real function.

Secondly, as Bultmann showed, the logical status of the 'I am' sayings is variable. Usually it is a recognition-formula, answering the question what something is. Thus in 6.35, 41, 48, 51 'I am the bread of life' explains what the bread under discussion is: it is Jesus himself. But it also carries with it the overtones of a qualificatory-formula, answering the question What are you? For by identifying the bread as himself, Jesus shows that he is himself the nourishment of the soul which the bread signifies. The same applies to 8.12; 10.7, 9, 11, 14; 14.6; 15.1, 5. 11.25 ('I am the resurrection and the life') is similar, but in this case it is the climax of the argument, because it constitutes the challenge to faith.

A different logic is required by 6.21, where *ego eimi* has no predicate, and so must be translated 'It is I'. This is a recognition-formula without the qualificatory aspect. In fact it is a direct quotation from the tradition (= Mark 6.50 exactly).

We are left with the six absolute uses of *ego eimi* in 8.24, 28, 58; 13.19; 18.5, 6. Apart from 8.58, these must also be translated 'I am he'. It is generally recognised that in 8.21-29 the discourse has allusions to the prophecy of Isa. 43.10-13. Here God declares himself to be the only Saviour, and the people are his witnesses so that all 'may know and believe and understand that I am he' (*ego eimi* in the Greek version). In other words he means 'I am the Saviour.' The same is true in John 8.24, 28, which form the climax of the discourse. Jesus points to himself as the agent of salvation. This also applies to 13.19.

There is, however, a further complicating factor. In Isa. 43.10, 13 God says 'I am he', and although the words in the Hebrew are different there is a real possibility that this is an allusion to God's revelation of his name in Exod. 3.14, 'I am who I am' (Greek version *ego eimi ho on*). What about Jesus in 8.24, 28? Is he claiming for himself the name of God? But this cannot be the proper meaning of the text here, which requires to be understood as 'I am he (i.e. the agent of salvation)', as we have just seen. The most that can be said is that John might have wished, by this choice of words and allusion to Isaiah, to suggest *also* that Jesus is the visible representative of God who bears this name.

But what about 8.58? Here there is an electrifying effect caused by the juxtaposition of past and timeless present tenses: 'Before Abraham was born, I am', i.e. exist. In fact this could be translated 'I am he' as before, meaning in this case 'I am the one who gives life' (cf. 8.51). But on the usual interpretation, which contrasts the birth of Abraham at a point in time with the timeless existence of Jesus as God's Son from eternity, the saying in its context means that Jesus can give life, because he has life in himself, being eternally existent. Even so, the text does not require a reference to Exod. 3.14, which again could be no more than an additional allusion, and cannot be proved to be John's intention.

Finally the *egō eimi* comes very impressively in the account of the arrest of Jesus in 18.5-8. In v. 5 Jesus simply identifies himself as the one whom the soldiers are seeking. But then, by a striking example of the evangelist's dramatic skill, this is repeated in v. 6 with a comment on the effect of Jesus' words: 'When he said to them, "I am he", they drew back and fell to the ground'. This surely is the effect of a theophany! But it still must be translated 'I am he' (as also in v. 8), though it perhaps carries the sense 'I am the agent of salvation', as in 8.28. The arrest begins the process of the act of salvation in which Jesus is revealed as the agent of salvation (13.19), and the aim of these verses is to show Jesus as in complete control of his destiny.

It remains true that the 'I am' sayings in John always make a great impression on readers of the Gospel, increasing the sense of the numinous and strange personality of Jesus. But for understanding John, it is necessary to be on guard against reading too much into them. In particular, it is a mistake to single them out as a basis for analysing the christology of John. In so far as they carry an allusion to Exod. 3.14, this is no more than what has been said in the Prologue in 1.14, 18, which provides a far better basis for understanding what the evangelist means.

The Resurrection

Jesus says 'I am he', and he means the Son of Man, who is lifted up on the cross, and whose crucifixion is also his glorification. This is the proper starting point for understanding John's treatment of the resurrection. The cross is central to the evangelist's theology of salvation, because it is the earthly act in which Jesus' glory as the Son of God is revealed and made accessible through the response of faith. The resurrection of Jesus is his transformation from death to glory, anticipating the transformation which all believers will share in the general resurrection (5.24-25; 11.21-27). The resurrection *stories* in chapters 20 and 21 are subordinate to this teaching as testimony. These stories all have a basis in the tradition, as we have already seen in considering the sources of the Gospel. But in each case John has built up the episode around a particular character in order to make a theological point, the necessity of believing in the risen Jesus without sight or touch.

From what we have seen of the evangelist's aims and methods, we should be ready to accept that none of these stories is a factual account of what actually happened. They are a careful reworking of stories which are themselves popular expressions of the proclamation of the resurrection, and have their own problems from the point of view of historical criticism. The earliest written evidence for the resurrection, however, is not the stories in the Gospels, but the statement quoted by Paul in 1 Cor. 15.3-7, which lists a series of appearances of Jesus, beginning with Peter. These verses begin with the important comment that 'Christ died for our sins according to the scriptures', which refers to the atoning death of Jesus and its foreshadowing in Scripture (Isaiah 53 and other passsages), which we have already considered. Then in v. 4 we are told that 'he was raised on the third day according to the scriptures'. This has important links with the Fourth Gospel, which show that John's teaching on the resurrection is anchored in the earliest tradition.

In the first place the idea of the third day, or three days, comes into the teaching of Jesus in two significant passages which link up with John. The first is Luke 13.32-33, in which Jesus speaks of his death as 'going away' (cf. John 7.33-36; 8.21-22), and uses the idea of three days idiomatically to represent a short space of time. This refers to the time required for him to complete his mission, which he is determined to continue in spite of the danger to his life. John applies this idea, using the phrase 'a little while', to the interval between Jesus' death and subsequent vindication (14.19; 16.16-19).

The other saying is Jesus' claim to be able to destroy the temple and build it in three days (Mark 14.58). Jesus probably did not mean it literally, but used it as a vivid way of expressing his absolute certainty of the vindication of his message of renewal in an incredibly short time. The saying is used as a taunt by the hostile crowd at the cross (Mark 15.29-30), which ironically applies it to his death and resurrection. John actually puts the saying into the mouth of Jesus himself in the account of the cleansing of the temple, which may well be its proper context (2.20). In the next verse it is said explicitly that it does not really mean the destruction and rebuilding of the temple (impossible at the time when John was writing), but 'the temple of his body' (v. 21).

In the second place the very same context refers to scriptural prophecy. Jesus' resurrection was 'according to the scriptures' (1 Cor. 15.4), and John 2.22 also points to the agreement of the words of Jesus with Scripture. This verse is a valuable vignette of the earliest Christian theology. For John tells us that the disciples remembered Jesus' words after his resurrection and discovered their true meaning by elucidating them in the light of Scripture. Reflection by the disciples after the resurrection is mentioned again in the account of the triumphal entry in 12.16, drawing attention to the agreement of memory and Scripture.

Thus the resurrection for the evangelist is a theological datum, quite apart from the resurrection stories. When we look again at the teaching on the passion with this fact before us, it becomes clear that the resurrection has coloured John's whole approach. Jesus will not only give his life, but 'take it again' (10.17). The lifting up of the Son of Man becomes his glorification (12.23; 13.31). His death will be immensely fruitful (11.52; 12.24). Though he dies, the disciples will see him again, though not in the way that the world sees (14.19-33). This is not a reference to resurrection appearances in a literal sense, but (as the context makes completely clear) the mutual indwelling of Jesus and the disciples which will be established permanently through the faith-relationship. The same idea is expanded in 16.16-24, promising a joyful relationship between the disciples and Jesus in glory.

The Paraclete

In the debates between Jesus and the unbelieving Jews, the evangelist has set out to show that Jesus surpasses the Law. But the Law remains always available, whereas Jesus has died and been withdrawn from view until his coming at the parousia. However the teaching on the resurrection has claimed that his withdrawal is to be seen in a positive light as the means of establishing a permanent relationship with him in glory. Clearly it is necessary to say something more about this relationship, if the argument is to be complete. This is the context of John's special teaching on the Holy Spirit.

The Spirit of God in the Old Testament is, like the Wisdom of God, an attribute of God himself, denoting his energy and creative power. It can be personified as a divine force, energising the great heroes and inspiring the prophets. In a society which thinks of angels and lesser spirits there is a tendency to make God's Spirit also a subordinate being of this kind. In Qumran, with its highly developed angelology, the Spirit of Truth is an angel opposed to the Spirit of Falsehood, who is the devil. In the Synoptic tradition Jesus has to distinguish his claim to be inspired by the Spirit of God from popular demonology (Matt. 12.24-32). The designation *Holy* Spirit (extremely rare in the Old Testament) came into currency in New Testament times to distinguish the Spirit of God from other spirits.

The Fourth Gospel has little use for angelology or demonology, but does reflect the Qumran type of dualism, with the devil as 'the father of lies' (8.44). But although the expression 'the Spirit of Truth' is used (14.17; 15.26; 16.13), this does not refer to a subordinate spirit, but to the Holy Spirit as the power of God himself. John's special interest is the inspiration of Christians who live in fellowship with the exalted Jesus. Here again we can see a basis in the tradition. The picture of earliest Christianity in Acts shows that the gifts of the Spirit and the powers of the age to come are already available. Paul explains that, sharing in the sonship of Jesus as

God's children, Christians have the constant help of the Spirit
(Rom. 8.12-17, 26-27). The way in which John makes this
point in 7.37-39 is disconcerting, because it seems to imply that
the Holy Spirit was not available at all (or did not even exist)
before Jesus was glorified. But what it really means is that this
function of the Spirit was not available before the completion of
Jesus' saving work.

It is in connection with this function that Jesus can be said to
be the giver of the Holy Spirit. This is expounded in the
discourses at the Last Supper (14.16-17, 26; 15.26–16.15).
Here it is shown that the Spirit will be the helper of the
disciples when they are persecuted for their faith. The idea is
enlarged further to include all the work of carrying forward
the mission of Jesus. There is a literary debt to the tradition
here (cf. Matt. 10.17-25, and the table of parallels in Brown, p.
694). This is where the unusual designation Paraclete
(*paraklētos*) comes in, which is variously translated advocate,
comforter, counsellor or helper. The legal sense of advocate is
probably basic in view of the function of the Spirit in the
tradition (cf. Matt. 10.19-20), but John uses the word more
broadly here. The point in John is that the Spirit is *another*
Paraclete (14.16), to act as helper to the disciples in place of
Jesus himself.

John's talk about the Paraclete has a strongly personal
colouring. Precisely because the continuing relationship with
Jesus in glory is a personal relationship, the power which he
gives to them, which is the power of God, can be no less
personal. There is no suggestion in John that the Spirit is an
impersonal divine power which can be manipulated by a
person whose heart is estranged from God.

Just as John's doctrine of incarnation had immense
influence on the subsequent development of christology, so also
the teaching on the Paraclete decisively affected the Christian
idea of the Holy Spirit as a *person* within the Godhead, thus
laying the foundation for the doctrine of the Trinity. But for
John it is not a matter of a metaphysical theory, but of
Christian experience which all believers can share.

Summary

John writes for people, whether friend or foe, whose idea of salvation in the religious quest is best expresssed with the words 'life' or 'eternal life'. In interpreting the gospel message in this way, the evangelist does not teach a realised eschatology in which the future is wholly absorbed in the present. The point is that the conditions of the future are available now, anticipating the future consummation, which still remains a valid concept in its own right. It was also observed that this is an intellectual rather than a political understanding of salvation. This probably reflects the social milieu of the readers.

Cutting across the social divide, the teaching of Jesus, Paul and John conveys a new dimension in the religious thought of the time, which is best expressed today as an enhancement of the idea of personal relationship. So for John the essential means of grasping salvation is to 'believe into' Jesus, which implies much more than intellectual assent to propositions about him. This is contrasted throughout the Gospel with a contemporary Jewish concept of the Law as the embodiment of the divine Wisdom and the means of eternal life.

Thus the Gospel is concerned with the qualifications of Jesus to be regarded as the means or agent of eternal life. In the Prologue and the discourses Jesus' capacity to achieve this purpose is contrasted with that of the Law, and he is found to have all the right qualifications. In addition to this contrast, John also builds on the contemporary conviction that the Scriptures are prophetic, revealing in advance God's plan of salvation, which is now in process of actualisation.

The Prologue shows both contrast and fulfilment in that, like the Law, Jesus is the embodiment of the pre-existent Wisdom/Word/Son of God, but surpasses and fulfils it. Reflecting the glory of God (like an only son of a father), he is the only real theophany of God, who is essentially beyond human sight.

The discourses attend to various aspects of salvation. It gradually becomes clear that the decisive difference between Jesus and the Law is the mutual indwelling of Jesus and the Father, and this is demonstrated supremely in his voluntary acceptance of the cross. So the death of Jesus is the climax of his revelation of the Father. It is at the same time the ultimate moral victory in which 'the prince of this world' is overcome. John's presentation of the death of Jesus in the passion narrative tones down the horror of crucifixion, emphasizing the fulfilment of Scripture, and Jesus' final word is 'It is finished' (*tetelestai*, 19.30). The saving work of God is thus accomplished.

In connection with the passion it was shown that John uses the designation Son of Man to refer to Jesus as the agent of a human act which reveals the divine glory. This human act is his death on the cross, which is both a literal 'lifting up' and at the same time his glorification. This provides the clue to John's idea of the resurrection, which is the new relationship with God established as a result of Jesus' death.

In the interval before the parousia Christians have the help of the Holy Spirit, the Paraclete. Though the teaching on the Holy Spirit in the Fourth Gospel is well in line with that of the New Testament in general, the insistence on the personal character of the Spirit is an important new emphasis, which has had profound consequences for Christian doctrine.

Further Reading

A straightforward account of the theology of the Fourth Gospel is given in W.G. Kümmel, *The Theology of the New Testament*, London: SCM, 1974. The treatment in R. Bultmann, *Theology of the New Testament*, vol. 2, London: SCM, 1955, has many penetrating insights, not too much affected by his unacceptable views on the origins of the Gospel. These are reflected, however, in E. Käsemann, *The Testament of Jesus*, London: SCM, 1968, which is a study of the theology of John in which Gnostic ideas are held to be basic. A critique of this book by G. Bornkamm (1968) is included in Ashton's *The Interpretation of John*. The positive exposition of the Johannine theology in R.T. Fortna, *The Fourth Gospel and its Predecessor*, Edinburgh: T. & T. Clark, 1989, is excellent even though in my view the reconstruction of the 'predecessor' and its theology is unconvincing.

On particular issues, christology is the subject of E.M. Sidebottom, *The Christ of the Fourth Gospel*, London: SPCK, 1961, and W.A. Meeks, *The Prophet-King: Moses Traditions and the Johannine Christology*, Leiden: E.J. Brill, 1967. Meeks' article, 'The Man from Heaven in Johannine Sectarianism', in the Ashton volume is also useful. The place of the Law in John's theology is treated by S. Pancaro, *The Law in the Fourth Gospel,* Leiden: E.J. Brill, 1975. See also G.J. Brooke, 'Christ and the Law in John 7–10', in B. Lindars (ed.), *Law and Religion: Essays on the Place of the Law in Israel and Early Christianity,* Cambridge: James Clarke, 1988, pp. 102-12. This theme is taken up in relation to John 6 by P. Borgen, *Bread from Heaven,* Leiden: Brill, 1965. The death of Jesus is treated by I. de la Potterie, *The Hour of Jesus: The Passion and Resurrection of Jesus in St. John,* New York: Paulist Press, 1989. The Son of Man in John is treated by F.J. Moloney, *The Johannine Son of Man,* Rome: LAS, [2]1978, and by B. Lindars, *Jesus Son of Man,* London: SPCK, 1983, ch. 9. The article by S.S. Smalley is 'The Johannine Son of Man Sayings', *NTS* 15, 1968-69, pp. 278-301. On the Holy Spirit see G. Johnston, *The Spirit-Paraclete in the Gospel of John,* Cambridge: CUP, 1970.

5

APPLICATION

'The Spiritual Gospel'

THE STUDY OF THE FOURTH GOSPEL needs to be done in depth in order to gain a true understanding of John. In the process preconceived ideas are challenged and have to be discarded, and new and unsuspected features of John's thought begin to emerge.

For most new students the first problem is to come to terms with the problem of historicity. John's narratives and dialogues are so vivid and circumstantial that at first sight they compel acceptance as eye-witness accounts. It takes time to realise that they were never intended to be historical reports. Too great a concern with historical problems is counter-productive, because it leads away from the more important task of understanding what John has to say.

It soon becomes apparent that the purpose of the Gospel could not have been achieved if it had been another volume of the same type as the Synoptic Gospels. The church fathers sensed this, and that is why Clement of Alexandria referred to it as 'the spiritual gospel'. The aim is to promote belief in Jesus as the Christ and Son of God so that 'you may have life in his name' (20.31). The words 'in his name' briefly point to the personal relationship of mutual indwelling between Jesus and the disciples which is essential teaching of the Gospel . The idea of 'life' as the object of the religious quest replaces the traditional preference for the kingdom of God, in accordance with the aspirations of the readers, whether Christians or unbelievers.

Thus the Gospel is concerned with historical tradition only in so far as it helps this spiritual purpose. Two other factors have dictated the form of the whole Gospel and set the parameters for the evangelist's approach. Firstly, to promote Christian faith in a milieu which was very different from that of the earliest church, it was necessary to show that the Christian claims about Jesus were anchored in the original tradition. Secondly, John must counter the claim that 'life' is available in the Law, and answer accusations that the Christian position is 'leading the people astray' by detaching them from the Law and amounts to 'blasphemy' in the status accorded to Jesus.

These two factors tend to create a tension between historical tradition and the current needs of theology. John solves it by making the tradition the starting-point for the theological construction. This explains the pattern of the discourses, which usually start with a traditional saying of Jesus providing the theological principle which is then worked out to a christological conclusion. However, apart from such individual sayings, the discourses must be the free composition of the evangelist, because they are concerned with aspects of christology which were simply not an issue previously.

Fundamentals of Faith

When we consider, however, the factors which account for the large element of creative writing in the Gospel, the biggest surprise is to find that the theology is far closer to the mainstream of early Christian teaching than appears at first sight. Most people are so dazzled by the Prologue that they assume that the Gospel is a new philosophizing interpretation of Christian faith all through. However, we have seen that the Prologue differs from the rest of the Gospel from a literary point of view, being deliberately modelled on the Wisdom poems. Its function is to give the rational basis of the positions which are taken for granted in the rest of the Gospel. In fact the point of the Prologue is to explain the crucial position of Jesus as the agent of universal salvation. This means that it supports the mainstream teaching about Jesus and his work of redemption.

John fully accepts the fact that the historic life and death of Jesus are indispensable. The outline of Jesus' ministry is used as the vehicle of the theology. The death of Jesus is given great prominence, because it is the key to the whole doctrine of salvation. Resurrection stories are retold, not only to complete the traditional pattern but also to point to the new relationship with God of the era of salvation. These items are presented in the light of the traditional concept of God's predetermined plan. John, in common both with contemporary strands of Judaism and the earliest Christian preaching, holds that the plan of salvation has been revealed in advance in the prophetic Scriptures, and is now in process of actualisation. It is fulfilled in the person of Jesus, and those who believe in him already experience the eternal life which belongs to the Last Day.

Where the Gospel seems most vulnerable, and in danger of losing grip on the traditional teaching, is in the handling of the divinity and humanity of Jesus himself. It is often felt that the Fourth Gospel suppresses the humanity of Jesus to such a degree that it becomes negligible from the point of view of salvation. In considering the Johannine church we have seen that it is very likely that this was actually how some of the members understood John. In modern times Käsemann has argued in *The Testament of Jesus* that the evangelist was in fact a docetist, regarding Jesus as a divine visitant, and using the tradition of his death merely as a means of expressing a spiritual truth.

However, the preceding pages should have persuaded readers that John accepts the full humanity of Jesus as historically true and theologically indispensable. Jesus has constant communion with God, and is himself the embodiment of God's Word/Wisdom/Son. Thus he is correctly referred to as the Son of God. But all his acts are human acts in which the Father's will is accomplished. The death of Jesus is the climax of these acts, and it is real. It is easy to describe John's account of Jesus in terms of a myth of the descent of a redeemer, who reveals the way of salvation and then returns to heaven whence he came. Quite apart from the fact that none of the myths of antiquity is exactly like this, for John the whole point is that in the case of Jesus this is no myth, but what was actually happening in his human life.

The Second Step

To see how to move beyond understanding to application, it may be helpful to compare an approach to the parables of Jesus which has come to be known as the New Hermeneutic. The basic observation is that the parables are not merely illustrative stories, but are stories which are effective in themselves. They perform the function of changing the hearers' perception of reality. Starting from conventional presuppositions, the story leads to a new perspective. A language-event has taken place, and the hearers will never see the matter in the old way again.

Bearing this observation in mind, we need to ask why the parables fail to make a similar impact on readers today. The reason is that our world-view and our presuppositions are so different from those of the original hearers. We thus have to think ourselves into the position of the original hearers as far as possible, so as to feel the parable's impact, before attempting to see what kind of application of it would be valid today. A well known example is the parable of the Pharisee and the Tax-collector (Luke 18.9-14). This fails to make its impact on modern readers, because we automatically identify ourselves with the tax-collector rather than the Pharisee, especially as we have inherited a false stereotype of the Pharisees as hypocrites. But the original hearers would have despised the tax-collector, making himself rich through extortion in the service of the hated Romans, and would have looked up to the Pharisee as an exemplary religious leader. It is in that setting that the parable would be a language-event to the hearers, changing their perception of God's scale of values.

Seeing the parable in these terms, however, is only the first step. For the hermeneutical process to be complete, the second step must be taken of applying this kind of fresh understanding to comparable circumstances today, in which our own ideas and interests may be presented with equally challenging observation.

Applying this method on a large scale to the Fourth Gospel, we can now see that the whole of our last chapter on 'Understanding John' was an extended example of the first step of thinking ourselves into the situation of the original readers. Placing ourselves alongside them, we listened to the Gospel as those whose concept of salvation is eternal life. We ranged ourselves alongside some who found the focus of their religion in the Law. But at the same time we were pulled by the whole presentation of the Gospel to side with the Christian readers, for whom Jesus is the focus of religion. The nature of eternal life, as presented by John, turned out to be a personal relationship with God mediated by Jesus' historic death and subsequent endless life, and made available through the faith-relationship with him.

The element of new realisation, which makes of the Gospel a language-event when it is read as far as possible through the eyes of the original readers, is John's treatment of the cross. In the crucifixion, which extinguishes Jesus' power to save himself, the climax of God's love in giving his Son is reached (3.16), and the union of the human Jesus and the divine Father is revealed (10.30). The lifting up of the Son of Man on the cross is also his glorification (13.31). It is the moment when God's plan of salvation is accomplished (19.30). The eye of faith can see this in the moment of human tragedy, and enter into fellowship with the one who so died.

The second step is to recognise that the historic events which lie behind the Fourth Gospel, and which are interpreted in this way by John, have symbolic value for the interpretation of life as it is experienced now. The Fourth Gospel has an existential dimension, because it is concerned with the problem of existence. For a modern reading the concept of 'life' as the goal of salvation might need revision. But it will stand for the deepest aspirations of every individual reader. The notion of an inadequate means of achieving these aspirations (represented in the Gospel by the Law) will correspond with the reader's own barriers to reality in facing fundamental issues through clinging on to anything less than the naked truth. The cross in John's presentation is not so much the shock to one's cherished certainties through the impact of inexplicable suffering, as the test of integrity in facing reality to the farthest limit. The sense of desertion is discovered to be union, and the moral victory over evil is won.

Integration

Some help in detailed application of the Fourth Gospel along these lines may be gained from current trends in literary criticism. Structural analysis, which has been developed in connection with narrative, can be applied to particular sequences of the Gospel, including the arguments of the discourses. The method exposes the dynamics of the narrative, showing how the author sets out the aim and the steps whereby that aim is achieved. By shearing off the visual details, the basic structures are exposed, which can then be seen to correspond with universal aspects of human experience.

Allied to this is the method of deconstruction, which aims to purge from the text the presuppositions which are brought to it by the assumptions of the reader. There is currently fashionable a 'hermeneutics of suspicion', which suspects any reading of a text which presupposes an orthodoxy or a stereotype as a key to interpretation. This is, however, a two-edged weapon. In seeking to remove the harm done to a text by the reader's unexamined presuppositions, the interpreter may impose fresh presuppositions which are equally misleading.

It is evident that work of this kind still belongs to the first step, which is the understanding of the text in itself. However the second step is not to be regarded as a separate activity, undertaken after all the work of understanding John has been completed. It is rather a fresh reading of the Gospel with full self-awareness. Having laboured to understand John through detailed critical study, and aware of one's own concept of salvation, one's own meaning of 'life', and one's own false substitutes for the truth, it is possible to read through the Gospel with intelligent appreciation, not being side-tracked into the wrong questions (such as the historical problems), but seeing it all objectively as John's presentation of Jesus, and at the same time subjectively aware of it as speaking to one's own understanding of existence. In this way objective study and present application are integrated into a single whole. The objective side is seen to be indispensable to understanding. It is not thrown aside as a fruitless and frustrating exercise. On the contrary it opens up the true riches of the Fourth Gospel and enables one to make them one's own.

Further Reading

The understanding of John in the first five Christian centuries is outlined by M.F. Wiles, *The Spiritual Gospel*, Cambridge: CUP, 1960, and more fully by T.E. Pollard, *Johannine Christology and the Early Church*, Cambridge: CUP, 1970. Modern literary approaches to the New Testament are presented in C.M. Tuckett, *Reading the New Testament*, London: SPCK, 1987, with useful bibliographies. The earlier book of John Barton, *Reading the Old Testament*, London: Darton, Longman & Todd, 1984, is especially helpful on these approaches, and can be used with profit by students of the New Testament. A helpful reading of John, which challenges the assumption that John is orientated entirely towards individual salvation and highlights the corporate dimension in relation to liberation theology, is D. Rensberger, *Overcoming the World: Politics and Community in the Gospel of John*, London: SPCK, 1988.

INDEX

INDEX OF BIBLICAL REFERENCES

INDEX OF AUTHORS